FRANCESCA DA RIMINI

ELEONORA DUSE
AS FRANCESCA DA RIMINI

FRANCESCA DA RIMINI

FRANCESCA DA RIMINI

By GABRIELE D' ANNUNZIO

TRANSLATED BY
ARTHUR SYMONS

WILDSIDE

Amor che al cor gentil ratto s'apprende . . .
Amor che a nullo amato amar perdona . . .
Amor condusse noi ad una morte.

Francesca da Rimini; Tragedia Gabriele D'Annunzio.

TO THE DIVINE
ELEONORA DUSE

INTRODUCTION.

"Francesca da Rimini" was acted for the first time at Rome, by Eleonora Duse and her company, on December 9, 1901. Has there, since "Hernani," been such a battle over a play in verse? The performance lasted five hours, and many of the speeches were inaudible on account of the noise in the theatre. Since then the play has been freely cut, it has been acted with the greatest success in the chief cities of Italy, and has raised more discussion than any play in verse of this century. The translation which follows has been made from the unabridged text.

The play is written in blank verse, but blank verse so varied as to be almost a kind of *vers libre*. This form of blank verse is not new in Italian. It is to be found in the pastoral tragedies of the Renaissance, in Tasso's "Aminta," in Guarino's "Pastor Fido." We need only open Leopardi to see almost exactly the same structure of verse. Take these lines of Leopardi ("Sopra un basso relievo antico sepolcrale"):

"Morte ti chiama; al cominciar del giorno
L' ultimo istante. Al nido onde ti parti
Non tornerai. L'aspetto
De' tuoi dolci parenti
Lasci per sempre. Il loco

A cui mova, è sotterra:
Ivi fia d' ogni tempo il tuo soggiorno."

Now take these lines, chosen at random from "Francesca":

"Ma giammai
m'eran fiorite, come in questo maggio,
tante, tante ! Son cento,
son più di cento. Guarda !
S' io le tocco, m' abbruccio.
Le vergini di Sant' Apollinari
non ardono cosi nel loro cielo
d'oro."

In English we shall find the most perfect example of blank verse varied into half-lyric measures in some of the choruses and speeches of "Samson Agonistes."

"But who is this? What thing of sea or land—
Female of sex it seems—
That so bedecked, ornate, and gay,
Comes this way sailing,
Like a stately ship
Of Tarsus, bound for the isles
Of Javan and Gadire,
With all her bravery on, and tackle trim,
Sails filled, and streamers waving,
Courted by all the winds that hold them play?"

Matthew Arnold, in "Empedocles on Etna," "The Strayed Reveller," and some of his most famous meditative pieces, has used the same metre, carrying his experiment indeed further, and playing with pauses in a more complicated way, not always, to my ear, with entire success. I am not sure that metre such as this can ever really become an English metre:

"Thou guardest them, Apollo!
Over the grave of the slain Pytho,

Though young, intolerably severe!
Thou keepest aloof the profane,
But the solitude oppresses thy votary,
The jars of men reach him not in thy valley,
But can life reach him?
Thou fencest him from the multitude:
Who will fence him from himself?

Mr. Henley has made for himself a rough, serviceable metre in unrhymed verse, full of twitching nerves and capable of hurrying or dragging.

"Space and dread and the dark—
Over a livid stretch of sky
Cloud-monsters crawling like a funeral train
Of huge primeval presences
Stooping beneath the weight
Of some enormous, rudimentary grief;
While in the haunting loneliness
The far sea waits and wanders with a sound
As of the trailing skirts of Destiny
Passing unseen
To some immitigable end
With her gray henchman, Death."

Now the essential difference between the metre of d'Annunzio and these other instances of a similar metre is that, with d'Annunzio, the metre is purely a means to an end, a dramatic end. He has aimed at giving variety and emphasis to blank verse, so as to make the verse render the speaker's mood with the greatest exactitude. Where, in ordinary blank verse, a single line is broken up into two or three small speeches, which have to be fitted into their five feet with an ingenuity which on the stage at least, goes for nothing, he lets his short lines stand more frankly by themselves And he moulds a long speech into greater flexibility, letting the voice pause on a single short line coming after longer lines, for emphasis, or running a short, unaccentuated line rapidly into the next, in a very effectual kind of *enjambement.* Yet, with all its variety, this metre is not, as is so much contemporary French *vers libre,* a vague, unregulated metre, which may be read equally as prose or as verse, and in which one has to search for the beat while one is reading it. The beat is always regular, clear, unmistakable. With the exception of a few dactylic passages, of which the most important occurs in the address to the fire, it is strictly iambic, and it is made of the normal verse of five feet, subdivided into verse of three feet and two feet.* As far as I recollect, the verse of four feet is never used, nor can I find a verse of four feet in the blank verse of Leopardi, though it is freely, and, I think, legitimately, used by every English experimenter in this metre. Italian verse, with its incessant elisions, its almost invariable double endings, lends itself, better than that of any other living language, to a metre which, in d'Annunzio's hands, becomes so easy, so much like prose, and yet so luxurious, so rich in cadence. In the translation which follows, I have of course rendered the double endings, for the most part, by single endings, using double endings at my discretion, as in ordinary English

* Sig. d'Annunzio writes to me: "I have added to the verse of eleven and of seven syllables, the verse of five, which is also iambic in structure. Thus the metre is formed of the hendecasyllable and of its two hemistichs (11–7–5.)."

blank verse. My version is literal, alike in words and rhythm, but my lines do not in every case correspond precisely with the lines of the original. They are intended to reproduce every effect of the original, as that can best be done in English verse, written on the principle of d'Annunzio's Italian verse.

In order to render the form of the original as closely as possible, I have often used weak endings which I should not have used had I been writing verse of my own. Take, for instance, these lines, which will be found on p. 25 of the Italian and also of the English :

> "Con qui parlavi ? Con le donne ? Come
> sei venuto ? Rispondi mi ? Sei tu
> di Messer Paolo Malatesta ? Su,
> rispondi !"

In my elisions I have tried to follow the example of the Italian as far as I could, without absolutely violating the principles of English verse, and, in short, I have done all I could to make a faithful copy, at the risk of leaving it "a mere strict bald version of thing by thing," which, Browning tells us in the preface to his translation of the "Agamemnon," is after all, what the reader of a translation should first of all look for and expect to find.

The motto of "Francesca da Rimini" might well be the line of Dante:

"Noi che tingemmo il mondo di sanguigno,"
and the play is more than a tragedy of two lovers, it is a study of an age of blood, the thirteenth century in Italy. In the real story, Paolo and Fran-

cesca were both married, she a mother and he a father of children, and it was only after ten years of marriage that Gianciotto surprised them together and stabbed them. Dante, in the fifth canto of the "Inferno," leaves out all but the bare facts of love and death. D'Annunzio refers once or twice to the wife, Orabile, but not to the children, nor does he leave any long interval between the beginning and end of the passion. But he gives us two people of flesh and blood, luxurious, pondering people, who love beautiful things, and dream over their memories; yet people who have no characteristics that might not have existed in an Italian man and woman of the thirteenth century. Paolo is a perfect archer, we see him shoot an arrow from the battlements, which, we are told later, has gone through the throat of one who mocked his brother to his face; we hear of his armour, his horse, as well as of his skill in music and the gentler arts. Francesca is full of tender feeling, and some of the most beautiful lines in the play are the lines which she speaks to her sister. But, as the man-at-arms on the battlements says of her:

> "Quella
> Non è già donna di paura."

She questions him about the Greek fire which he is stirring in a cauldron, and lights one of the fiery staves, indifferent to the danger, intent only on the strange, new, perilous beauty. She is exalted by the sight of the blood-red roses growing in the sarcophagus, and she cries to the roses. Violent deeds go on around her wherever she is. In her father's house brother fights with brother, and it is her brother's bleeding face which appears to her through the barred window, with ominous significance, at the close of the first act, as she sees Paolo for the first time, and offers him a rose. In the house of her husband she sees fighting from the walls, and her husband's brother, Malatestino, is brought in wounded in the eye. There is a prisoner whose cries come up from the dungeons underground, while Malatestino, who is afterwards to betray her to her husband, persecutes her with his love. She hates cruelty, but like one to whom it is a daily, natural thing, always about her path.

> "To fight in battle is a lovely thing,
> But secret slaying in the dark I hate,"

she says to her husband, as she tells him of his brother's thirst for blood. Towards her husband her attitude is quite without modern subtlety; he has won her unfairly, she is unconscious of treachery towards him in loving another; she has no scruples, only apprehensions of some unlucky ending to love. And when that ending comes, and the lover is caught in the trapdoor, as he is seeking to escape, and the husband pulls him up by the hair, and kills them both, the husband has no moralising to do; he bends his crooked knee with a painful movement, picks up his sword, and breaks it across the other knee

The action of the play moves slowly, but it moves; behind all its lyrical outcries there is a hard grip on the sheer facts of the age, the definite realities of the passion. D'Annunzio has learnt something from Wagner, not perhaps the best that Wagner had to teach, in his over-amplification of detail, his insistence on so many things beside the essential things, his recapitulations, into which he has brought almost the actual Wagnerian "motives." When the moment is reached which must, in a play on this subject, be the great moment or the moment of failure, when the dramatist seems to come into actual competition with Dante, d'Annunzio is admirably brief, significant, and straightforward. In the scene in which "Galeotto fu il libro, e chi lo scrisse," he has made his lovers read out of the actual book out of which Dante represents them as reading, the old French romance of "Lancelot du Lac," and the words which they repeat are the actual words of the book, put literally into Italian.

It is not any part of my purpose to compare "Francesca da Rimini" with Mr. Stephen Phillips' "Paolo and Francesca," but, after translating this scene, I had the curiosity to turn to the corresponding scene in the English play. The difference between them seemed to be the difference between vital speech, coming straight out of a situation, and poetising round a situation. In d'Annunzio you feel the blind force and oncoming of a living passion; and it is this energy which speaks throughout the whole of a long and often delaying play. Without energy, "la grâce littéraire suprême," as Baudelaire has called it, beauty is but a sleepy thing, decrepit or born tired. In "Francesca da Rimini" beauty speaks with the voice of life itself.

Arthur Symons.

DRAMATIS PERSONÆ

DRAMATIS PERSONÆ.

OSTASIO. BANNINO. FRANCESCA. SAMARITANA.	Sons and Daughters of Guido Minore da Polenta.
BIANCOFIORE. ALDA. GARSENDA. ALTICHIARA. ADONELLA. The Slave.	Francesca's Women.
SER TOLDO BERARDENGO. ASPINELLO ARSENDI. VIVIANO DE' VIVII. BERTRANDO LURO. An Archer.	Partisans of Guido.
GIOVANNI, "The Lame," known as GIANCIOTTO. PAOLO "The Beautiful." MALATESTINO "The One-eyed."	Sons of Malatesta da Verrucchio.
ODDO DALLE CAMINATE. FOSCOLO D'OLNANO. Archers. Men-at-Arms.	Partisans of Malatesta.

The Merchant. The Merchant's Boy. The Doctor. The Jester. The Astrologer. The Musicians. The Torchbearers.

SCENE: *At Ravenna, in the House of the Polentani; at Rimini, in the House of the Malatesti.*

FRANCESCA DA RIMINI

ACT I.

A Court in the House of the Polentani, adjacent to a garden that shines brightly through a marble screen, pierced in the form of a transept. A loggia runs round it above, leading on the right to the women's apartments. and in front, supported on small pillars, affords a double view. On the left is a flight of steps leading down to the threshold of the enclosed garden. At the back is a large door, and a low, barred window, through which can be seen a range of arches surrounding another larger court. Near the steps is a Byzantine sarcophagus, without a lid, filled with earth, like a flower pot, in which grows a crimson rosebush.

The WOMEN *are seen, leaning over the loggia, and coming down the stairs, gazing curiously at the* JESTER, *who carries his viol hanging by his side, and in his hand an old jerkin.*

ALDA.

Jester, hey, Jester!

GARSENDA.

Adonella, Adonella, here is the Jester
In the court! O Biancofiore,
The Jester ! he has come !

ADONELLA.

Are the gates open yet ?

BIANCOFIORE.

Let's make the Jester sing.

ALDA.

Hey, tell me, are you that Gianni . . .

JESTER.

Sweet ladies . . .

ALDA.

That Gianni who was coming from Bologna ?
Gian Figo ?

GARSENDA.

Are you Gordello who is coming from Ferrara?

JESTER.

Dear ladies . . .

ADONELLA.

What are you seeking there ?

JESTER.

The trail of the scent.

BIANCOFIORE.

We brew in limbecs oils of lavender,
And oils of spikenard.

JESTER.

I am no apothecary's pedlar, I.

ALTICHIARA.

You shall have a bunch though, my good nightingale,
If you will sing.

GARSENDA.

Look at him, how he droops!

JESTER.

Fair ladies, have you . . .

BIANCOFIORE.

Yes,
Heaps upon heaps.

ADONELLA.

Bags full
And coffers full of it. Madonna Francesca
Can dip her beauty, if she has a mind to,
In oil of lavender.

JESTER.

I thought rather to find the smell of blood
In the house of Guido.

ALDA.

Blood of the Traversari : in the streets,
In the streets you will find it.

ALL.

Polenta! Polenta! Down with the Traversari!

JESTER.

Heigho! Catch who catch can, go free who may!
The sparrows are becoming sparrow-hawks.

[*Shouts of laughter ring down the staircase, between the twi-horned head-dresses.*]

ALL.

Grapple with the Ghibelline!

JESTER.

Be quiet now, don't let the archer near you,

Or he will fetch me suddenly such a bolt
As will lay me out my length for all my life.

ALDA.

You swear you are a Guelph?

JESTER.

By San Mercuriale of Forlì
(That sets the belfry crumbling on the pate
Of the Feltran people) I tell you I am Guelph,
As Guelph as Malatesta da Verrucchio.

GARSENDA.

Good then, you are safe; only be circumspect:
You have leave to smell.

JESTER.

To smell? And not to eat?
I am a dog, then?
How many bitches are there in the place?
Let's see.

[*He goes down on hands and feet like a dog, and makes for the women.*]

GARSENDA.

Ah nasty dog!

ALDA.

Filthy dog!

ALTICHIARA.

Wicked dog!
Take that!

JESTER.

Ahi, ahi, you have smashed my viol,
You have broken my bow.

ADONELLA.

Take that!

GARSENDA.

And that!

BIANCOFIORE.

And that!

JESTER.

They are all in heat!
I would I knew which one of you the most!

[*They all strike him on the back with their fists, laughing. And as the* JESTER *jumps about amongst them like a dog, they begin to dance round him, shaking out their perfumed skirts.*]

BIANCOFIORE.

Take hands, and dance a round!

ADONELLA.

Do you smell the spice,
Lavender and spikenard?

ALTICHIARA.

I am flame and ice,
I am flame and ice!

BIANCOFIORE.

Fresh in cool linen is sweet lavender!

ALDA.

Come in, bright eyes, into my garden fair!

ALTICHIARA.

An odour comes, no garden can I find.

ADONELLA.

How comes this lovely odour on the wind?

ALL.

Smell! Smell!

GARSENDA.

Sweet shift that long in lavender has lain;

Sweetheart, the time of May has come again.

ALL.

Smell! Smell!

ADONELLA.

I would I had my sweetheart near my side,
And nearer than my shift is near to me.
Dear love is dear to me!
Dear love is dear to me!

ALL.

Smell! smell! smell!

JESTER

[*Standing up and trying to catch one of them*].

Catch who catch can!
If I catch one of you. . .

[*With cries of laughter, they run up the stairs then stand panting with merriment.*]

ALDA

[*With a contemptuous gesture*].

You are no sheep dog, you!

GARSENDA.

You are a pantry dog,
Poor Jester! have you not
More stomach now for food than bantering?

JESTER

[*Scratching his throat*].

May be I have. I dined some while ago.
Fine scents fill no lean paunches.

GARSENDA.

Well then, well,
Go rather to the Archbishop Bonifazio,
He is the biggest glutton

That eats in the world: the Genoese. This house
Is Guido da Polenta's.

JESTER.

Yellow with flower of the black hellebore,
Because there is no juniper in the world,
May all be salt to me,
Ravenna women have it . . . in the round,
Salt be to me!

GARSENDA.

Round-pated you yourself!
You thought to get the better of us, eh?
We have got the better of you.

BIANCOFIORE.

Sing, Jester!

ALDA.

Dance, Jester!

JESTER

[*Picking up his rag*].

You have pulled me all to pieces,
Mischief o' me! Have you, by chance, a little. . .

GARSENDA.

A little bacon?

JESTER.

Have you a little scarlet?

ADONELLA.

Are you for jesting with us? We are ready.

BIANCOFIORE.

But who are you? that Gianni. . .

ALTICHIARA.

O, Biancofiore, look what clothes he has!
The doublet is at loggerheads with the hose.

GARSENDA.

He is Gian Figo, who was coming from Bologna.

BIANCOFIORE.

Come from Bologna without a bolognino.

ALDA.

I am sure he is of the Lambertazza party.

GARSENDA.

An evil race!

ALDA.

He has been put to shame
By the Geremei.

ALTICHIARA.

Have you not lost a princedom, noble sir?

GARSENDA.

O, Adonella, look at him: he has fled
In nothing but his trousers.

JESTER.

And you will have them off me.

ADONELLA.

What a poor thing! Look at yourself in the glass,
As crooked as a cross-bow on its stock.

BIANCOFIORE.

Now you will sing the spoiling of Bologna,
And how King Enzo was made prisoner.

GARSENDA.

Have I not told you he is from Ferrara?

JESTER

[*Impatiently*].

I am from Ferrara and I am from Bologna.

GARSENDA.

Was it then you
Who escorted from Bologna to Ferrara
Ghisolabella de' Caccianimici
To the good Marchese Opizzo?

JESTER.

Just so, just so, 'twas I, just as you say.

GARSENDA.

It was you too who made
The match between the sister of the Marquese
And that old and rich judge, him of Gallura,
A shrivelled, wizened thing
That had the help of his big man-servant?

JESTER.

Just so, 'twas I, just as you say; and I had
In thanks for it. . .

ALDA.

A bone?

ADONELLA.

Two chestnuts?

BIANCOFIORE.

Three
Walnuts and a hazel-nut?

ALTICHIARA.

A stump of pimpernel?

GARSENDA.

A pair of snails
And an acorn?

JESTER.

This mantle that you see, of Irish frieze?
No; or of purple Tyrian samite? no;

But all of velvet crimson-coloured, lined
With skins of miniver.

GARSENDA.

Look, look, Altichiara,
The thing he is holding!

ALTICHIARA.

A little threadbare cloak.

GARSENDA.

No, no, it is a Romagna jerkin.

ALDA.

Then
You are Gordello, you are not Gian Figo.

ADONELLA.

But no, he is a Jew.

BIANCOFIORE.

He is the huckster Lotto
Of Porto Sisi.

ALTICHIARA.

Sells fripperies and songs.

ADONELLA.

What have you with you? Have you rags or ballads?

JESTER.

Fool that I am, I thought to find myself
In the palace of the nobles of Polenta,
And here I am in a chirping nest of swallows.

GARSENDA.

Comfort yourself, I am satisfied by now
That I have taught you, Master Merrymaker,
Ravenna women are not easily beaten
At the game of banter.

JESTER.

And of the pole, too.

ALDA.

You chuckle over it?

ADONELLA.

Will you whet your whistle?

BIANCOFIORE.

No, Alda: come now, make him sing to us.

GARSENDA.

Do you not see the sorry sort of viol
He trails here, Adonella?
It seems to me a sort of pumpkin cowled,
With its big belly and its monstrous neck.
The rose is meanly cut,
Here's a peg missing, here
The bass and tierce are gone.
Well, if he barks, his viol gapes in answer.
Go, scrawl arpeggios
Upon a rebeck, let the bow alone.

BIANCOFIORE.

You let the joke alone, then, Mona Berta.
Let us see now if he knows how to sing.
Come on then, Jester,
And sing us, if you can, a pretty song.
Do you know any of that troubadour
Who calls himself the Notary of Lentino?
Madonna Francesca knows a lovely one
Beginning this way: "Very mightily
Love holds me captive." Do you know the song?

JESTER.

Yes, I will say it now,
If you have a little scarlet.

ALTICHIARA.

But what is it you want then, with your scarlet?

ADONELLA.

We are waiting, we are waiting!

JESTER.

I want you, if you will,
To put a patch for me
Upon this jerkin.

ALTICHIARA.

What a mad idea,
To patch Romagna woollen, and with scarlet!

JESTER.

I pray you, if you have it, do for me
This service. There is one tear here, in front,
Another on the elbow; here it is.
Have you two scraps?

ALTICHIARA.

I will put it right for you
If you will sing to us.
But I assure you, 'tis a novelty
To set the two together.

JESTER.

I go about in search of novelties,
As novel as myself:
That's just the reason.
But not long since I found a novelty,
As I was on my way:
I met with one,
Not two miles out of here,
That had his head of iron,
His legs of wood, and talked with both his shoulders.

BIANCOFIORE.

This is a novelty in very deed,
But tell us how.

ADONELLA.

We are waiting! we are waiting!

JESTER.

Listen, and I will tell you. I met with one
That wore an iron headpiece on his head
And went to gather fir-cones in the wood
Here at Ravenna, and he went on crutches,
And when I asked him had he seen about
A little friend of mine, he shrugged his shoulders,
Saying by this means
He had not seen him.

BIANCOFIORE
[*contemptuously*].

But this is a true thing.

JESTER.

Am I not novel,
That tell true things for fables? Catch who catch can!
So, you will do then what I asked of you?
And after you have done it,
You shall wait no great while before you learn,
The occasion offering, that Gian Figo. . .

GARSENDA.

Ah!
You have let it out at last.

ALL.

He is Gian Figo!

JESTER.

Before you learn Gian Figo is as wise
As Dinadan the King of Orbeland's son,
That found his wisdom by forgetting love.

ALTICHIARA.

But now enough of this: time for a song!

BIANCOFIORE.

"There comes a time to rise . . . "
Do you not know the song King Enzo made,
The King that lost his kingdom in a battle
Against Bologna, and was put in prison
In a big iron cage, and ended his life there,
Singing his sorrows?
Seven years ago in March: I can remember.
"There comes a time to rise, a time to fall,
A time for speaking and for keeping silence."

ADONELLA.

No, no, Gian Figo,
Tell us instead the song
Made by King John, John of Jerusalem,
"For the flower of all the lands."

GARSENDA.

No, tell us that of good King Frederick,
"A song of pure delight."
(Madonna Francesca, the flower of all Ravenna
Knows it) made for the flower
Of Soria when the sire of Suabia
Loved a most worthy maiden
His wife had brought with her from over sea,
And brought to honour; and this wife of the King
Of Suabia was no other than the daughter

Of John, King of Jerusalem, and her name
Was Isabella, and she died, and then
King Frederick took for his wife the sister
Of the simple Henry of England; and he loved
her
Exceedingly, because, like our Madonna
Francesca, she was skilled
In music, and all ways of lovely speech;
And this was the third wedding; and she, then,
That sang and played all day and all night long,
Had . . .

[BIANCOFIORE *covers her mouth with her hand.*]

JESTER.

What a bibble babble! O poor King Enzo,
There never is a time here to be silent.
What's to be done with all your merchandise,
Gian Figo, chitter, chatter, chattering,
Here are four voices, and more like a thousand!

ALTICHIARA.

Listen to me now, Jester. Let the King
Alone. He is dead and buried. Say instead
" O mother mine,
Give me a husband." " Tell me why, my
child."
" That he may give me happy. . . "

ALDA.

That is old!
Listen to me, Jester.

ALTICHIARA.

Then, " Monna Lapa,
She spun and span. . ."

ALDA.

No!

ALTICHIARA.

Then: "O garden-close,
I enter and nobody knows."

ALDA.

Hush!

ALTICHIARA.

Then: "Let's all
Have seven lovers,
That's one for every day of the week."

ALDA.

Hush!

ALTICHIARA.

Then:
"Monna Aldruda, don't be a prude, a
Piece of good news. . ."

ALDA.

O hush! Biancofiore,
Do shut her mouth. Jester, listen to me:
These are old songs. . .

ADONELLA.

There's a new troubadour
Known at Bologna: surely you have heard him?
He's the new fashion;
They call him Messer Guido. . . Messer Guido
Di . . . di . . .

JESTER.

Di Guinizello.
He was one that went out with the Lambertazzi,
Took refuge at Verona, and there died.

ALDA.

Good, let him die: he's for the Emperor.
May he go now and make his rhymes in hell!

Listen to me, Jester; tell us a story
Of knights.

BIANCOFIORE.

Yes, yes, the knights of the Round Table!
Do you know their stories?
The love of Iseult of the golden hair?

JESTER.

I know the histories of all the knights
And all the knightly deeds of chivalry
Done in King Arthur's time,
And specially I know of Messer Tristan
And Messer Lancelot of the Lake, and Messer
Percival of the Grail, that took the blood
Of our Lord Jesus Christ, and of Galahad,
And of Gawain, and the rest. I know them all.

ALDA.

Of Guenevere?

ADONELLA.

Good luck, Jester, good luck!
We will tell Madonna Francesca what you know,
Will we not, Alda?
She takes delight in them;
Jester, she will reward you bountifully.

JESTER.

She will give me the remainder . . .

ADONELLA.

What remainder?

JESTER.

Why, the two scraps of scarlet.

ADONELLA.

She will give you
Quite other gifts, the bountifullest gifts.

Rejoice that she is marrying;
Messer Guido marries her to a Malatesta;
The wedding day is close at hand.

BIANCOFIORE.

Meanwhile
Tell us a story: we are all ears. "There is time
To listen," said the prisoner.

[*They group themselves about the* JESTER, *leaning towards him: he begins.*]

JESTER.

How the fay Morgana sent to Arthur's Court
The shield foretelling the great love to be
Between good Tristan and the flower-like Iseult;
And this shall be between the loveliest lady
And the most knightly knight in all the world.
And how Iseult and Tristan drank together
The draught of love that Iseult's mother, Lotta,
Had destined for her daughter and King Mark.
And how the draught of love, being perfect, brought
Both these two lovers to one single death.

[*The women stand listening, the* JESTER *preludes on the viol and sings.*]

"*Now, when the dawn of day was nigh at hand,*
King Mark of Cornwall and good Tristan rose. . ."

THE VOICE OF OSTASIO
[*behind the scenes*].

Tell him, the Puglian thief,
Tell him, I say, that I will wash my hands
And feet in his heart's blood!

ALDA.

Messer Ostasio!

GARSENDA.

Come away, come, come!

[*They scatter, and rush up the stairs, with laughter and cries, and along the loggia.*]

JESTER.

My jerkin, my good jerkin! I commend you,
My jerkin, and the scarlet!

ALTICHIARA

[*leaning over the loggia*].

Come back at noon:
It shall be ready.

OSTASIO DA POLENTA *enters by the great door at the back, accompanied by* SER TOLDO BERARDENGO.

OSTASIO

[*seizing the terrified* JESTER].

What are you doing here, rascal?
Whom were you talking with, the women? How
Did you come here? Answer me, I say. Are you
From Messer Paolo Malatesta? Now,
Answer!

JESTER.

O sir, you are holding me too hard.
Ahi!

OSTASIO.

Did you come here with Messer Paolo?

JESTER.

No, sir.

OSTASIO.

You lie!

JESTER.

Yes, sir.

OSTASIO.

You were talking with
The women; what did you say? something, no doubt,
Concerning Messer Paolo. What was it?

JESTER.

No, sir, no, sir, only of Messer Tristan.

OSTASIO.

Take care; you do not trifle with me twice,
Or you shall keep this tryst of yours with Tristan
Longer than you intend, unseemly fool.

JESTER.

Ahi, ahi! what have I done to vex you, sir?
I was only singing something.
I was only singing a song of the Round Table.
The ladies asked me for a history
Of knights. . . I am a Jester and I sing
From hunger, and my hunger
Hoped better things than beating in the house
Of the most noble Messer Guido. I,
That keep no hack, have footed
From the Castle of Calbeli
All the way here: I left
Messer Rinieri fortifying his keep
With some seven hundred strong
Of infantry.

OSTASIO.

You come from Calbeli?

JESTER.

Yes, sir.

OSTASIO.

Were you ever with the Malatesti
At Rimino?

JESTER.

No, sir; never, sir.

OSTASIO.

Then
You do not know Messer Paolo, the Beautiful,
That dotes on jesters, and would have them sing
And play at all times in his company?

JESTER.

Unluckily I do not know him, sir,
But I would gladly know him. And if I find him,
I pray to be found always at his side.
Long life to Messer Paolo Malatesta!

[*He is about to retire hastily.* OSTASIO *catches hold of him again, and calls the* ARCHER *who is on guard in the other Court.*]

OSTASIO.

Jacomello!

JESTER.

What have I done, and why
Do you do me violence?

OSTASIO.

Too much talk.

JESTER.

I am mute.
It is hunger barking in me. Keep me prisoner
In the kitchen, and I will be as still as oil.

OSTASIO.

Will you be silent, rascal? Jacomello!
I give this prattle-seller to your charge,
See that you bit and bib him.

JESTER.

A spice cake,
Give me a spice cake.

OSTASIO.

Give him a box on the ears.

JESTER

[*As the* ARCHER *thrusts him out*].
When Madonna Francesca knows how you have used me. . . .
I am to sing at her wedding.
Long life to Messer Paolo Malatesta!

[*Raging, and full of suspicion,* OSTASIO *draws the* NOTARY *towards the sarcophagus.*]

OSTASIO.

These jesters and the like men of the Court
Here in Romagna are a very plague,
Worse than the Emperor's rabble. They are tongues
Of women; they know everything, say everything;
They go about the world

Spreading abroad their news and novelties;
Their ears are at the keyholes of us all.
Who wants to know how the good Papal Rector
Lay with the wife of Lizio da Valbona?
Who wants to know
How much Rinieri da Calbeli has taken
Out of the purses of the Geremei?
As for this rascal
That gossipped with the women of Francesca,
If he had been a jester
Of the Malatesti
By now the women had heard all the news
There is to tell of Paolo,
And all the cunning plan had been vain,
Ser Toldo, that you counselled
Out of your manifold wisdom.

SER TOLDO.

As for him,
He was so poor and threadbare,
How could I take him for a follower
Of such a lordly knight as Paolo,
He being so bountiful
With gentry such as these?
But you are well-advised in bitting him.
These creatures of the Court
May be by way of being soothsayers,
And often steal the trade
Of the astrologers.

OSTASIO.

True. And this slave
Of Cyprus, that my sister loves so dearly,
I have my doubts of her; she too, I think,
Is something of a soothsayer; I know

That she interprets dreams. The other day
I saw my sister full of heavy thoughts,
And almost sorrowful,
As if some evil dream had come to her;
And only yesterday
I heard her heave such a long, heavy sigh
As if she had a trouble in her heart,
And I heard Samaritana
Say to her: "What is it, sister? Why do you weep?"

SER TOLDO.

Messer Ostasio, it is the month of May.

OSTASIO.

In truth there is no peace for us until
This marriage is well over. And I fear,
Ser Toldo, lest some scandal come of it.

SER TOLDO.

Yet you know well, what sort
Of woman is your sister, and how high
Of heart and mind. If she see this Gianciotto,
So lamed and bent, and with those eyes of his,
As of an angry devil,
Before the marriage-contract
Be signed and sealed, why, neither will your father
Nor you, nor any, of a certainty
Bring her to take
The man for husband, not although you set
Your dagger at her throat, or haled her through
Ravenna by the hair.

OSTASIO.

I know it well, Ser Toldo, for my father

Gave her for foster-mother
A sword of his of a miraculous edge,
That he had tempered in Cesena blood
When he was Podestà.

SER TOLDO.

Well then, I say,
If this be so, and you desire the match,
There is no other way to compass it.
And seeing that Paolo Malatesta comes
As procurator of Gianciotto here,
And with full powers
For the betrothal of Madonna Francesca,
I say you should proceed
Instantly to the marriage,
If you would sleep in peace, Messer Ostasio.
Paolo is a fair and pleasant youth,
And makes a brave decoy,
Undoubtedly; yet it is far too easy
To learn that he is married to Orabile.
And you, did you not beat this jester but
For fear of idle talk?

OSTASIO.

Yes, you are right,
Ser Toldo; we must put an end to this.
My father is returning from Valdoppio
This very night; we will have all prepared
And ready for to-morrow.

SER TOLDO.

Very good,
Messer Ostasio.

OSTASIO.

Yet . . . What will come of it?

SER TOLDO.

If you do all, as all this should be done,
With secrecy and prudence, Madonna Francesca
Will find out nothing till at Rimino,
She wakes, the morning after
Her wedding day, and sees
Beside her . . .

OSTASIO.

Ah, it is like some vile revenge!

SER TOLDO.

And sees beside her rise
Gianciotto.

OSTASIO.

O, she is so beautiful!
And we avenge ourselves upon her beauty,
Almost as if she wronged our house and us
In coming to be born
Here like a flower in the midst of so much iron.
We are giving her to the lame Malatesta
For the sake of that poor hundred infantry!
But is she not herself
Worth more than all the lordship of Romagna?
False notary, how did you poison first
My father's mind? All this
Is your base bargaining. I will not have it.
Do you understand?

SER TOLDO.

Why, what tarantula bites you,
Messer Ostasio?
Surely you will not find
A better match to make in all Romagna?

OSTASIO.

The Malatesti? Who then after all
Are these Verrucchio folk? By this alliance
Shall we have got Cesena,
Cervia, Faenza, Forlì, Civitella,
Half of Romagna?
A hundred infantry!
To hunt the Traversara region, O
The mighty succour!
And Dovadella, and Zello, and Montaguto
Already in our power perhaps. Gianciotto!
But who is he, Gianciotto? When I think
How that Traversarian widow,
That ancient scabby bitch, has mated with
(After the nephew of the Pope) the son
Of Andrea, the King of Hungary. . . .

SER TOLDO.

What is the King of Hungary to you?

OSTASIO.

But here are we, with this
Puglian clodhopper,
This Guglielmetto that now vaunts himself
As the legitimate heir
Of Paolo Traversari,
And harries us; and we shall never break him
With this mere hundred infantry, and he
Will surely come again with help from Foglia.
What shall we hope for then
From Malatesta?

SER TOLDO.

Malatesta is the chief of all the Guelphs
Now in Romagna, and the chief defender

Of the Church, and he has the favour of the Pope,
And he was made the governor of Florence
Under King Charles, and whosoever seeks
A captain. . . .

OSTASIO.

Notary.
Guido di Montefeltro shattered him,
Once, at the bridge of San Procolo. Notary,
Guglielmino de' Pazzi drove him back
At Reversano, and has made him since
Give up the fortress of Cesena.

SER TOLDO.

Ay,
But the victory at Colle di Valdelsa
Against the Sienese,
The time he slaughtered Provenzan Salvani?
But when he made Count Guido prisoner
On the borders of Ancona, and brought him back,
Him and his men, to Rimino? But when
He intercepted
The famous secret letters
From the Emperor Baldwin to King Manfred? Come,
In truth it seems to me,
Messer Ostasio,
Your memory is then no longer Guelph.

OSTASIO.

If the Devil comes to me and lends me a hand
That I may root and ruin the evil race
Of the slave Pasquetta and the Puglian hag,
I am for the Devil, notary.

SER TOLDO.

Ah, ah! I guessed the truth:
It is the tarantula of Puglia bites you.

OSTASIO.

The Emperor Frederick (God, for this thing
Grant him a cup of water down in hell!)
Had utterly destroyed the seed of them,
When he hurled Aica Traversari headlong
Into the fiery furnace.
And lo, one day there comes into Ravenna
A certain slave, Pasquetta, with her sweetheart,
And tells you: "I am Aica,"
And comes on one Filippo, an Archbishop,
And he affirms her the legitimate heir,
And with the taking over of the Dukedom
Makes her the lady mistress! And from that
The filthy vagabond of a husband holds
The headship of the very Ghibelline party
Against the house of Polenta! O Ser Toldo,
Now we are doing deeds of chivalry
Against Guglielmo Francisio, bastard
Of shepherd-folk. Do you understand?

SER TOLDO.

But you,
Have you not driven him out of Ravenna?

OSTASIO.

With the infantry of Gianciotto Malatesta?

SER TOLDO.

You are ungrateful, Messer Ostasio.
Gianciotto Malatesta in two days
Broke all the bars and gratings in the streets;
Between Sant' Agata and Porta San Mamante,

He massacred the gang
Of the Anastagi;
Between San Simone and Porta San Vittore
His heavy cross-bolts cleared
The whole pack in a breath.
Nor is he ever one to spare himself,
But proved his courage,
There, with a buckler braced about his arm,
A rapier in his hand ;
And always in the crush
Set on his priceless horse,
A raging beast that gave his enemies
What travail more he could, so that he had
Always some dozen more or less of men
Under his horse's hoof; and Stefano
Sibaldo, that stood by,
Swears, when the Lamester does
A feat of arms, it is beautiful to see him;
He is a master in the art of war!

OSTASIO.

O Ser Toldo, you had certainly your share
Of the booty! You will take away their skill
From those who sang the song of the twelve barons
Of Charlemagne,
Lord of the flowing beard. How much, I pray,
Came to your share?

SER TOLDO.

The tarantula of Puglia
Is a certain sort of spider,
That brings all kinds of luck to those he bites.
I am not now, alas,
All that I have been once!

But the Malatesti always have been ill
Bearers of shame, and now Gianciotto knows
The way by which one gets inside the walls
Here at Ravenna. . . . But you might give your sister,
No doubt, to the Prince Royal of Salerno,
Or to the Doge of Venice.

OSTASIO
[*absorbed*].

Ah! is she
Not worth a kingdom? How beautiful she is!
There never was a sword that went so straight
As her eyes go, if they but look at you.
Yesterday she was saying: " Who is it
You give me to?" When she walks, and her hair
Falls all about her to her waist, and down
To her strong knees (she is strong, though very pale)
And her head sways a little, she gives forth joy
Like flags that wave in the wind
When one sets forth against a mighty city
In polished armour. Then
She seems as if she held
The eagle of Polenta
Fast in her fist, like a trained hawk, to fling him
Forth to the prey. Yesterday she was saying:
" Who is it you give me to?"
Why should I see her die?

SER TOLDO.

Now you might give your sister
To the King of Hungary
Or better, to the Paleologue.

OSTASIA.

Be silent,
Ser Toldo, for to-day
I am not patient.

THE VOICE OF BANNINO.

Ostasio! Ostasio!

OSTASIO.

By God! here is Bannino, here is the bastard
That pants and lolls his tongue.
I knew it.

BANNINO *appears at the door at the back of the stage, panting and dishevelled, like a fugitive, with* ASPINELLO, ARSENDI, VIVIANO DE' VIVII, *and* BERTRANDO LURO, *who are bleeding and covered with dust.*

BANNINO.

Ostasio!
The men of Forlì have attacked the waggons
Of salt, by Cervia;
They have put to flight the convoy and overturned
The waggons.

OSTASIO

[*Shouting*].

Ah, I knew it!
But they have not cut your throat?

ASPINELLO.

The Ghibellines that were exiled from Bologna,
With those too of Faenza and Forlì

Gather in companies over all the land
And are laying all things waste with fire and sword.

OSTASIO.

Jesu our Lord, good tidings for your Vicar!

VIVIANO.

And they have burned Monte Vecchio, Valcapra,
Pianetto. They have laid waste Strabatanza and Biserno
For Lizio da Valbona,
They have laid waste, for the Count
Ugo da Cerfugnano,
The country of Rontana and of Quarmento.

OSTASIO.

God of mercy, still good tidings,
Good tidings to thy servants, and good tidings!

BERTRANDO.

Guido di Montefeltro
Takes horse to Calbeli
With engines, and balistas;
And he will have the castle.

OSTASIO.

More! more!
Christ Jesus, to thy praise always!

VIVIANO.

There was Scarpetta
Of the Ordelaffi with the Forlì folk.

BANNINO.

They have put to flight the convoy and overturned
The waggons and taken cattle

And horses, and have killed
Malvicino da Lozza
And many soldiers, and made prisoner
Pagano Coffa; and the others in disorder
Have fled in search of safety towards the sea.

OSTASIO.

And you, you towards the land,
As fast as horse could carry you. I knew it
I knew it well.
Where did you leave your sword?
And you have thrown away your helmet too.
Save himself he who can! That is your cry.

BANNINO.

My sword? I broke my sword
In the very rage of striking blows with it.
There were three hundred, maybe four, against us.
Aspinello, Bertrando,
Say, both of you, and you
Viviano, say if I did well or no.
I had against me more than twenty men
That would have taken me; and I carved my life
With my own hand out of their flesh and bone.
Say, all of you!

OSTASIO.

You see
They cannot answer for you; they are tasked
To stanch the flowing of their blood, and wipe
The dust away that clings about their faces.
But you are clean, you; cuirass, sleeves, all clean,

Spotless. Your enemies
Had got no veins then in their bodies? You
Have not a scratch upon your whited face,
O mighty man of valour in your words!
[*The* THREE SOLDIERS, *taking their harness off their backs, and wiping it, move away.*]

BANNINO

Ostasio! Ostasio! Enough!

OSTASIO.

I knew it well,
I had but laughter when
My father picked you out
To lead the waggon safely in. I said:
"May the good Bishop of Cervia
Preserve him with his crozier! In Ravenna
'Tis very certain we shall have no salt."
Did I say wrong? Go, go, Bannino, go
And mince the lungs of hares into a dish
For sparrow-hawks.

BANNINO.

You should be silent, you,
While I was in the fray,
Stayed safe at home, plotting with notaries.

OSTASIO.

O lord and leader of harlots, you shall know
That if the men of Forlì did not catch you,
Because you were too nimble,
'Tis I will catch you.

BANNINO.

What? with treachery,
After your fashion?

OSTASIO.

I will do it so that you,
This time at least, do not go whimpering home
To tell my father.

SER TOLDO.

Peace! peace!

BANNINO.

I will tell him
Something I know, this time.

OSTASIO.

What do you know?

BANNINO.

You know the thing I mean.

SER TOLDO.

Peace, peace, O peace!
Be brothers!

OSTASIO.

He is from another nest.

SER TOLDO.

Messer Ostasio, he is but a boy.

OSTASIO.

Speak then, if you know how to wound a man
At any rate with your tongue.

BANNINO.

You know the thing
I mean. I keep my counsel,

OSTASIO.

No, pour out
Your gall, that is now painted in your face,
Or I will wring you up as if I wrung
A wet rag out.

BANNINO.

Ostasio,
I am not so skilled in pouring out my gall
As you your wine
With an unshaken hand.

OSTASIO.

What wine?

BANNINO.

Your wine, pure wine, pure wine, I mean.

OSTASIO.

Listen to me, bastard!

BANNINO.

Our good old father
Fell sick one day. With what a tenderness
You watched about him, O you best of sons!
Do you know now? do you know? I know a thing
That you too know.
God dry your right hand up!

OSTASIO.

Ah, what a woman's lie is that! O bastard,
Your day has come at last;
No use in flying from the enemy!

[*He draws his sword and rushes upou* BANNINO, *who leaps aside and avoids the blow. He is about to follow him, when* SER TOLDO *tries to draw him back.*]

SER TOLDO.

Messer Ostasio, what is it you would do?
Let him alone! Let him alone! He is
Your brother. What would you do to him?

[*The* SLAVE *comes out on the loggia and watches.*]

BANNINO

[*terrified*].

O father,

O father, help! Francesca, O sister, help!
No! you will kill me. Wretch! Wretch! No, no, pardon,
Ostasio! No, I will not tell . . .

[*Seeing the point at his throat, he kneels down.*]

The poison
Was not yours.

[*The* THREE SOLDIERS, *unarmed, have come back.*]

No, I will not tell! O pardon!

[OSTASIO *wounds him in the cheek. He swoons.*]

OSTASIO.

Nothing, nothing, it is nothing.

[*He leans over and looks at him.*]

It is nothing;
He has fainted; I have only pricked the skin;
Not in a bad place, no; and not in anger.
I pricked him just a little
That he might learn not to fear naked steel,
That he might bear him better in the fray
And not lose sword and helmet
When he turns tail next on the Ghibelline.

[*The* THREE SOLDIERS *lift* BANNINO.]

Take him away to Maestro Gabbadeo,
And let his wounds be staunched
With salt out of the Cervia salt-mines.

[*He watches the wounded man as he is borne away, then closes the great door with a clang. The* SLAVE *silently retires from the loggia.*]

Come,
Ser Toldo, let us go.

SER TOLDO.

What will your father
Say when he comes?

OSTASIO.

My father
Is much too kind to this young bastardling.

[*He looks gloomily on the ground.*]

He is from another nest, and he was hatched
Not by the eagle, no, but by a jay.
Did you not hear what he was stuttering?
About a wine, a wine . . . [*He pauses grimly.*]
It was a stock
Suborned by some one of the Anastagi.
Christ guard my father and my house from traitors!

SER TOLDO.

And Madonna Francesca then?

OSTASIO.

Yes, we will give her
To the Malatesta.

SER TOLDO.

May God prosper it!

OSTASIO.

The vengeances that wait for us are great
And many, and some tears shall flow in the world,
Please God, more bitter than the salt in all
The salt-mines of this Cervia. Come with me,
Ser Toldo, Paolo Malatesta waits.

[*They go out.*]

The SLAVE *reappears, carrying a bucket and a sponge. She comes down the stairs in silence, barefooted. She looks at the bloodstains on the pavement and goes down on her knees to wash them up. From the rooms above is heard the song of the* WOMEN.

CHORUS OF WOMEN.

Ah me, the sorrow of heart
In the heart that loves too well. Ah me!
Ah me, if the heart could tell
How love in the heart is a flame. Ah me!

[FRANCESCA *and* SAMARITANA *are seen coming out on the loggia side by side, with their arms about each other. The chorus of* WOMEN *follows them, carrying distaffs of different colours; but pauses on the lighted loggia, standing as in a singing gallery, while the two sisters go down the stairs to the level of the garden. The slave, having washed out the stains, hurriedly pours the bloodstained water in her bucket into the sarcophagus among the flowers.*]

FRANCESCA

[*pausing on the stairs*].

It is love makes them sing!

[*She throws back her head a little, as if abandoning herself to the breath of the melody, light and palpitating.*]

WOMEN.

Ah me, the sorrow and shame,
In the sad heart on the morrow Ah me!

FRANCESCA.

They are intoxicated with these odours.
Do you not hear them? With a sighing fall
Sadly they sing
The things of perfect joy.

[*She withdraws her arm from her sister's waist, and moves a little away, pausing while the other takes another step downward.*]

WOMEN.

Ah me, the bitter sorrow.
All life long. Ah me!

FRANCESCA.

Like running water
That goes and goes, and the eye sees it not,
So is my soul.

SAMARITANA

[*With a sudden alarm, clinging closer to her sister*].
Francesca,
Where are you going, who is taking you?

FRANCESCA.

Ah, you awaken me.

[*The song pauses. The* WOMEN *turn their backs, looking down into the other court. They seem to be on the watch. The twi-horned headdresses and the tall distaffs shine in the sun, and now and then there is a whispering and rustling of lips and garments in the clear sunlight.*]

SAMARITANA.

O, sister, sister,
Listen to me: stay with me still! O stay
With me! we were born here,
Do not forsake me, do not go away,

Let me still keep my bed
Beside your bed, and let me still at night
Feel you beside me,

FRANCESCA.

He has come.

SAMARITANA.

Who? Who has come
To take you from me?

FRANCESCA.

Sister, he has come.

SAMARITANA.

He has no name, he has no countenance,
And we have never seen him.

FRANCESCA.

It may be
That I have seen him.

SAMARITANA.

I have never been apart
From you, and from your breath;
My life has never seen but with your eyes;
O, where can you have seen him, and not I
Seen him as well?

FRANCESCA.

Where you
Can never come, sweetheart, in a far place
And in a lonely place
Where a great flame of fire
Burns, and none feed that flame.

SAMARITANA.

You speak to me in riddles,
And there is like a veil over your face.
Ah, and it seems as if you had gone away,

And from far off
Turned and looked back; and your voice sounds
to me
As out of a great wind.

FRANCESCA.

Peace, peace, dear soul,
My little dove. Why are you troubled? Peace;
You also, and ere long,
Shall see your day of days,
And leave our nest as I have left it; then
Your little bed shall stand
Empty beside my bed; and I no more
Shall hear through dreams at dawn
Your little naked feet run to the window,
And no more see you, white and barefooted,
Run to the window, O my little dove,
And no more hear you say to me: "Francesca,
Francesca, now the morning-star is born,
And it has chased away the Pleiades."

SAMARITANA.

So we will live, ah me,
So we will live forever;
And time shall flee away,
Flee away always!

FRANCESCA.

And you will no more say to me at morn:
"What was it in your bed that made it creak
Like reeds in the wind?" Nor shall I answer
you:
"I turned about to sleep,
To sleep and dream, and saw,
As I was sleeping, in the dream I dreamed. . ."

Ah, I shall no more tell you what is seen
In dreams. And we will die,
So we will die forever;
And time shall flee away,
Flee away always!

SAMARITANA.

O Francesca, O Francesca, you hurt my heart,
And see, Francesca,
You make me tremble all over.

FRANCESCA.

Little one, peace,
Peace, be at rest.

SAMARITANA.

You told me of the dream
You dreamed last night, and while
You spoke I seemed to hear
A sound of voices calling out in anger,
And then a cry, and then
The sound of a door shutting; and then silence.
You did not finish telling me your dream,
For then
The women began singing, and you stopped;
And you have left my heart in pain for you.
Whom is it that our father gives you to?

FRANCESCA.

Sister, do you remember how one day
In August we were on the tower together?
We saw great clouds rise up out of the sea,
Great clouds heavy with storm,
And there was a hot wind that gave one thirst;
And all the weight of the great heavy sky
Weighed over on our heads; and we saw all

The forest round about, down to the shore
Of Chiassi, turn to blackness, like the sea;
And we saw birds flying in companies
Before the murmurs growing on the wind.
Do you remember? We were on the tower;
And then, all of a sudden, there was dead
Silence. The wind was silent, and I heard
Only the beating of your little heart;
And then a hammer beat,
As by the roadside some flushed plunderer,
Hot for more plunder, bent
Shoeing his horse in haste.
The forest was as silent as the shadow
Over the tombs;
Ravenna, dusk and hollow as a city
Sacked by the enemy, at nightfall. We,
We two, under that cloud
(Do you remember?) felt as if death came
Nearer, yet moved no eyelid, but stood there,
Waiting the thunder.

[*She turns to the* Slave, *who stands motionless beside the sarcophagus.*]

O Smaragdi, who,
Who was it, in the song among your people,
That stood, shoeing his horse under the moon,
And when his mother spoke to him, and said:
"My son, I pray you take not in your course
The sister when you take the brother, nor
Lovers that love each other with true love,"
Answered her sourly back:
"If three I find, three I take; if I find
Two, I take one; and if I find but one,
I take the one I find"?
What was the name they gave him in your land?

SLAVE.

An evil name
It is not good for any man to name.

FRANCESCA.

Tell me, what will you do without me here,
Smaragdi? What is there that I can leave you
When I go hence?

SLAVE.

Three cups of bitterness
Leave me:
The first that I may drink at early morning;
The second, on the stroke
Of mid-day; and the third,
Soon after vespers.

FRANCESCA.

No, I will not leave
Three cups of bitterness, but you shall come
With me, Smaragdi, to the city of Rimino,
And you shall be with me, and we will have
A window opening upon the sea,
And I will tell you over all my dreams,
Because you see unveiled
The face of sorrow and the face of joy;
And I will speak to you of that most sweet
Sister, my little dove;
And you will stand, and, looking through the window,
See all the skiffs and galleys on the sea,
And you will sing: "My galley of Barbary,
What is the port you make for, and the shore
Where you would anchor? Cyprus I would make for,
And at Limisso anchor,

And land my sailors for a kiss, my captain,
For love!" Come now, must I not take you with me
To Rimino, Smaragdi?

SLAVE.

To go with you
It were a happiness to tread on thorns,
And to pass through the flames
To be with you.
You are the heaven with stars,
The sea with waves.

FRANCESCA.

The sea with waves!
But tell me, what are you doing with the bucket,
Smaragdi?

SLAVE.

I have watered
The roses.

FRANCESCA.

Why then have you watered them
Out of their season? Why? Samaritana
Will be angry with you. She
Gives water to the roses
As soon as the bell sounds for vespers. Come,
What do you say, Samaritana?

SAMARITANA.

I
Would let them die, because,
Francesca, you are going away from us.

FRANCESCA.

O beautiful, and perchance
A holy thing, being born in this most ancient

Sarcophagus that was the sepulchre
Perchance of some great martyr or of some
Glorious virgin!

[*She walks round the sarcophagus, touching with her fingers the carvings on the four sides.*]

The Redeemer treads
Under his feet the lion and the snake;
Mary saluted by Elizabeth;
Our Lady, and the angel bids "All hail!"
The stags are drinking at the running brook.

[*She stretches out her arms towards the rose-tree.*]

And now the blood of martyrdom reflowers
In purple and in fire. Behold, behold,
Sister, the ardent flame,
Behold the roses that are full of fire!
Here did our own hands plant them, on a day,
It was October, on a day of battle
That crimsoned the red eagle of Polenta.
Do you remember? How the trumpets sounded
From Porta Gaza to the Torre Zancana,
As the new flag unfurled,
The flag our father
Had bid us make for him with forty yards
Of crimson cloth: it was a mighty flag-pole.
Do you remember?
And we had broidered round about the hem
A border fringe of gold.
It conquered! And from then
We held these roses
To be a blessed thing, we held them spotless
And undefiled as a white virginal robe;
And there was never plucked
One of these roses, and three springtides through

They blossomed into flower and fell to dust
In the sarcophagus.
But never have they flowered until this May,
Such floods, such floods of them.
There are a hundred. Look!
They burn me if I touch them.
The virgins vowed to Saint Apollinaris
Burn not with such an ardour in their heaven
Of gold. Samaritana,
Samaritana, which of them say you
Found here a sepulchre
After her glorious martyrdom? O, which
Of these was sepulchred
Here, tell me, here, after her martyrdom?
Look, look: it is the miracle of the blood!

SAMARITANA

[*Frightened, drawing her towards herself*].
Sister, what is it, sister?
You speak as if you raved.
What is it? Speak!

BIANCOFIORE.

[*From the loggia.*] Madonna Francesca!

ADONELLA.

Madonna
Francesca!

FRANCESCA.

Who calls for me?

ADONELLA.

Come up here! O come quick!

ALDA.

Here, here, Madonna Francesca, come up here
And see!

ADONELLA.

Come quickly. It is your betrothed
Who is passing.

BIANCOFIORE.

He is passing through the court,
He is with your brother, Messer Ostasio;
And here too is Ser Toldo Berardengo,
The notary, he is with them.

ALDA.

Here, here! Madonna Francesca, come up quickly.
He is there, he is there!

[FRANCESCA *goes hastily up the stairs.* SAMARITANA *is about to follow her, but stops, overcome.*]

ADONELLA.

[*Pointing him out to* FRANCESCA *who leans over to look.*]
See, there is he who comes
To be your husband.

GARSENDA.

O most happy lady,
Most happy lady,
He is the fairest knight in all the world,
In very truth. See now
How his hair falls, and waves about his shoulders
In the new way, the Angevin way!

ALDA.

And how
Well made he is, a proper man, well girded
About the surcoat with the hanging sleeves
That almost touch the ground.

ALDA.

And what a splendid clasp and what an aglet!

BIANCOFIORE.

And tall! And slender! And a royal carriage!

ADONELLA.

And how his teeth are white!
He smiled a little, and I saw them glitter.
Did you not see, did you
Not see?

GARSENDA.

O, happy, happy shall she be
That kisses him on the mouth!

FRANCESCA.

Be silent.

ALDA.

He has gone. He is passing now
Under the portico.

[*The* SLAVE *opens the grating, closes it furtively behind her, and disappears into the garden.*]

FRANCESCA.

Be silent, be silent!

[*She turns, covering her face with both her hands; when she withdraws them, her face appears transfigured. She goes down the first stairs slowly, then with a sudden rapidity throws herself into the arms of her sister, who awaits her at the foot of the staircase.*]

ALTICHIARA.

Messer Ostasio is coming back alone.

BIANCOFIORE.

The slave, where is she going? She is running
Down through the garden.

GARSENDA.

Smaragdi runs and runs
Like a hound unleashed. Where is she going?

ADONELLA.

Sing
Together, sing the song of the fair Isotta:
" O date, O leafy date! . . . "

[*The women form into a circle on the loggia.*]

CHORUS OF WOMEN.

O date, O leafy date,
O love, O lovely love,
What wilt thou do to me?

[FRANCESCA, *held close in her sister's arms, suddenly begins to weep. The chorus breaks off. The* WOMEN *speak together in low voices.*]

BIANCOFIORE.

Madonna weeps.

ADONELLA.

She weeps!

ALDA.

Why does she weep?

ALTICHIARA.

She weeps because her heart is sick with joy.

GARSENDA.

Straight to the heart
He wounded her. If she is beautiful,
He is beautiful, the Malatesta!

ADONELLA.

Born

One for the other
Under one star.

GARSENDA.

O happy he and she!

ALDA.

Long may he live who crowns
Their heads with garlands!

BIANCOFIORE.

First rain of the season
To the corn brings increase;
And the first tears of love
To the lover bring peace.

ADONELLA.

She smiles, she smiles
Now.

BIANCOFIORE.

And her tears
Laugh like the hoar-frost.

GARSENDA.

Go, warm the bath,
Get the combs ready.

]*The* WOMEN *scatter over the loggia, with their garments fluttering, nimble as birds on the bough, while the tall staves of their distaffs pass and repass, shaken like torches against the blue strip of the sky. Some go into the rooms and come out again. Others stand as if watching. And they talk in subdued voices and they move without sound of footsteps.*]

BIANCOFIORE.

These smelling-bottles
Of bright new silver
We have to fill
With water of orange flower and water of roses.

ALDA.

We have to fill
Four mighty coffers
With sheets of linen fringed with silken lace.

ALTICHIARA.

And stores of pillows
We have wrought for a marvel.
We have wrought so many
That never in dreams the people of Rimino
Have seen such store!

ADONELLA.

Ah, we have much to be doing!

GARSENDA.

And we must fold the quilts
Of cloth of linen
And all the embroidered coverlets of gold.

BIANCOFIORE.

And count the nets and ribbons for the hair
And all the girdles and the belts of gold.

ADONELLA.

We have much to be doing!

GARSENDA.

I take my oath
A better dowry brings to Malatesta

The daughter of Messer Guido than the daughter
Of Boemondo, King of Servia,
To the Doge of Venice.

ADONELLA.

And if she go by sea we have store enough
Of oil and lavender
To perfume all the sea.

ALDA.

And we will teach the women.
Of Rimino, that are a little raw,
The art of odours.

BIANCOFIORE

And the art of playing.
And of singing and of dancing.

ALTICHIARA.

O, I forgot
That I have yet to put a patch of scarlet
On the jerkin of Gian Figo.
He comes again at noonday.

BIANCOFIORE.

He will do well to finish
The story of Morgana and the shield,
And of the magic potion.

ALDA.

Hey, hey, the wedding in May!
The table must be laid for thirty dishes
And for a hundred trenchers.

BIANCOFIORE.

We must bring word
To Mazarello
To have the music ready.

ADONELLA.

Ah, we have much to be doing!

GARSENDA.

Hey, hey, to work, to work!

ADONELLA.

Come, lay our distaffs down
And take our garlands up.

[*They go into the room with a murmur, like a swarm of bees into the hive.* FRANCESCA *has raised her head, and her tears are suddenly lit up by a smile. While the* WOMEN *on the loggia were chattering in a low voice among themselves, she wiped the tears from her face and the face of her sister with her fingers. Now she speaks, and her first words are heard through the last words of the* WOMEN.]

FRANCESCA.

O sister, sister,
Weep no more. Now I weep no more. See now,
I am smiling. Tears and smiles
Are not enough now. Close
And narrow is the heart to hold this power,
And weeping is a virtue all outspent,
And laughter is a little idle play;
And all my life seems now,
With all the veins of it,
And all the days of it,
And all old things in it, far away things,
From long ago in the old time, the blind
And silent time, when I
Was but an infant on my mother's breast,

And you were not,
Seems all to tremble
In one long shuddering
Over the earth;
And now through all the streams
That laugh and weep in the places
That I have never known,
The forces of my being are cast abroad;
And I hear the air cry with a terrible cry,
And I hear the light
Sound like a trumpet-peal,
And the shouting that I hear
And the tumult cry out louder than the sound
In days of vengeance, sister, when the blood
Colours the portals of our father's house.

SAMARITANA.

O Francesca, my Francesca, O dear soul,
What have you seen? What is it you have seen?

FRANCESCA.

No, do not be afraid!
What is it your eyes speak?
What sickness am I stricken with, and what,
What have I seen?
It is life runs away,
Runs away like a river,
Ravening, and yet cannot find its sea;
And the roar is in my ears.
But you, but you,
Take me, dear sister, take me with you now,
And let me be with you!
Carry me to my room,
And shut the shutters fast.
And give me a little shade,

And give me a draught of water,
And lay me down upon your little bed,
And with a covering cover me and make
A silence of the shouting, make a silence
Of the shouting and the tumult
I hear within my soul!
Bring stillness back to me,
That I may hear again
The bees of May
Beat on the window, and the cry of the swallows,
And some of your soft words,
Your words of yesterday,
Your words of long ago
And long ago,
Out of an hour that comes to me again
Like an enchantment.
And hold me close, dear sister,
And hold me close to you!
And we will wait for night
Night with its prayer and sleep,
Sister; and for the morning we will wait
That brings that morning-star.

GARSENDA

[*rushing in upon the loggia*].

He is coming, he is coming! O Madonna
Francesca! see, he is coming by the way
Of the garden. I have seen him from the room
Of the coffers, I have seen him
Under the cypresses. Smaragdi shows him
The way.

[*The other* WOMEN *join her, curious and mirthful; and they have garlands on their heads for joy: and they have with them three* GIRLS, *lute-players and viol-players and flute-players.*]

FRANCESCA

[*white with fear, and beside herself*].

No, no, no! Run,
Run, women, run!
Let him not come! Run, run!
Women, go out to meet him,
Let him not come! Shut to
The gates, and bar the way, and say to him
Merely that I salute him! and you, you,
Samaritana, help me,
Because I cannot fly; but my knees fail
And my sight fails me.
But you, my women, run,
Run now, and meet him,
And bid him turn again! Go out to meet him,
And say that I salute him!

THE WOMEN.

He is here!
He is here, he is here at hand!

[*Aided by her sister,* FRANCESCA *is about to go up the stairs; but suddenly she sees* PAOLO MALATESTA, *close to her, on the other side of the marble screen. She stands motionless, and he stops, in the midst of the arbutuses; and they stand facing one another, separated by the railing, looking at one another, without word or movement. The* SLAVE *is hidden behind the leaves. The* WOMEN *on the loggia form in a circle, and the* PLAYERS *sound their instruments.*]

CHORUS OF WOMEN.

Over the land of May
The archer with his band
Goes out to seek his prey.
At a feast of fears,
In a far-off land,
A heart sighs with tears.

[FRANCESCA *leaves her sister and goes slowly towards the sarcophagus. She picks a large red rose, and offers it to* PAOLO MALATESTA *across the bars.* SAMARITANA *with bowed head goes up the stairs weeping. The women take up the song. At the barred window, at the back,* BANNINO *appears, with his face bandaged; then drawing back, he beats at the door closed by* OSTASIO. FRANCESCA *trembles.*]

THE VOICE OF BANNINO.

Francesca, open, Francesca!

ACT II.

A cross-shaped room, in the house of the Malatesti, with projecting side beams and strong pillars, two of which, at the back, support an arch which leads through a narrow closed entrance between two walls pierced by loopholes, to the platform of a round tower. Two side staircases of twelve steps run from the entrance to the leads of the tower; a third staircase, between the two, runs from the leads to the floor underneath, passing through a trap-door. Through the archway are seen the square battlements of the Guelfs, provided with blockhouses and openings for pouring down molten lead. A huge catapult lifts its head out of its supports and stretches out its framework of twisted ropes. Heavy crossbows, with large-headed, short, and square bolts, balistas, arco-balistas, and other rope-artillery, are placed around, with their cranks, pullies, wheels, wires, and levers. The summit of the tower, crowned with engines and arms that stand out in the murky air, overlooks the city of Rimino, where can be dimly seen the wing-shaped battlements of the highest Ghibelline tower. On the right of the room is a door; on the left, a narrow fortified window looking out on the Adriatic.

In the closed entrance is seen a MAN-AT-ARMS *stirring the fire under a smoking cauldron. He has piled against the wall the tubes, syphons and poles of the fiery staves and darts, and heaped about them all sorts of prepared fires. On the tower, beside the catapult, a young* ARCHER *stands on guard.*

MAN-AT-ARMS.

The meadow of the Commune is still empty?

ARCHER.

As clean and polished as my buckler.

MAN-AT-ARMS.

Still
Not a soul stirring!

ARCHER.

Not the shadow even
Of a Gambancerro or of an Omodeo.

MAN-AT-ARMS.

They seem then to be dead already, those
That have to die.

ARCHER.

Quite otherwise than dead!
If all we did not buckle breastplates well,
And if the gates were not cross-bolted fast,
You would soon hear a hammering of hearts
In the regions about Rimino. . . . Ah, there goes
A donkey.

MAN-AT-ARMS.

It is Messer Montagna, eh?
Of the Parcitadi, or Messer Ugolino
Cignatta.

ARCHER.

Both of them, my Berlingerio,

Stand with the right foot ready
In the stirrup of the crossbow, for the sign
To come out and to face the bolts and bars.

MAN-AT-ARMS.

What sign? The Parcitade
Lacks his astrologer. He waits and hopes
For succour from Urbino.
But long before Count Guido comes to us,
By the body of San Giulian the martyr,
We shall have burnt the city to the ground.
We have enough to do with burning down
Half of Romagna. 'Tis warm work this time,
I warrant you! The Lamester
Wanted to singe his horse's mane with one
Of these fire-bearers:
Sure sign we are in salamander weather.

ARCHER.

He loves the stench of singeing, it would seem,
More than the civet of his wedded wife,
That woman of Ravenna! another thing
Than firebrands or this sulphur and bitumen!
A smile of hers would set the city alight
And all the country and the territory.

MAN-AT-ARMS.

She smiles but little. She is always overcast
With thinking, and with anger. She is restless.
I see her almost every day come up
Upon this tower. She scarcely speaks. She watches
The sea, and if she sees
Some galley or some frigate on the sea,
She follows it with her eyes
(Blacker than pitch, her eyes!)

Until it fades away,
As if she waited for a message or
Longed to set sail. She goes
From tower to tower,
From the Mastra to the Rubbia,
And from the Gemmana to the Tanaglia,
Like a lost swallow. And sometimes I fear,
When she is on the platform,
That she will take a flying leap and fall.
Misericordia!

ARCHER.

The Lamester is well made
To ride astride upon the Omodeo,
To batter strongholds, and to ford the streams,
And to force palisades,
To plunder and to pillage all the earth,
But not to labour in the lovely vineyard
That God has given him.

MAN-AT-ARMS.

Hush! You must not speak
So loud; we should not hear him if he came.
He goes about more softly than a panther,
You cannot hear him when he comes. He makes
A goodly pair with Messer Malatestino,
That comes upon you always suddenly
Without your knowing how or whence he came,
And gives you the same start,
Always, as if you had come upon a ghost.

ARCHER.

This is the day we are to lay about us.
The women will be all shut up.

MAN-AT-ARMS.

This one

Is not a lady to be frightened. Look,
See what is stirring.

ARCHER

[*returning to his post*].

I see the friars,
The hermits of Sant' Agostino, pass
To the exorcising. I can smell the stench
Of singeing in the cool air.

MAN-AT-ARMS.

And the gate
Of the Gattalo is closed still?

ARCHER.

Ay, closed still.
Our men, that had to come Verrucchio way,
Will be by now with trumpets and flags flying
At the bridge of the Maone. Messer Paolo
Came with the infantry by the postern gate
Of the sea.

MAN-AT-ARMS.

The mixture now
Is ready brewed. Since midday I have stirred
The ladle, mixed and moulded it together.
We are to sling barrels and casks of it
Upon the excommunicated houses.
But what is it we wait for? The conjunction
Of Mars with Venus? This astrologer,
Come from Baldach, does not quite seem to me
A modern Balaam. God be on our side!
Look if you see him now
Upon the belfry of Santa Colomba.
He is to ring the bell three times, to say
The fates are in our favour.

ARCHER.

I can see
A great long beard.

MAN-AT-ARMS.

May he be tarred all over with his tow,
And brayed into a mortar! I suspect him.
He was with Ezelino at Padua,
And other of hell's own Ghibellines. I know not
Why Messer Malatesta
Keeps in his company.

ARCHER.

Guido Bonatto, of Forlì, I know
To be a true astrologer of battles.
I saw him on the great day of Valbona,
And his prognostic never faulted.

MAN-AT-ARMS.

Now
The cursed Feltran has him. Thunder strike
His eyesight and his astrolabe!

[FRANCESCA *enters by the door on the right, and advances as far as the pillar that supports the arch. She wears about her face a dark band that passes under her chin and joins a kind of skull-cap that covers her hair, leaving visible the tresses knotted on her neck.*]

ARCHER.

The dust
Begins to rise over toward Aguzano.

MAN-AT-ARMS.

Are they Count Guido's horsemen
That ought to come from Petramala?

ARCHER.

No.

May God cast down their eyes
Out of their visors into the dust!

MAN-AT-ARMS.

But who,

Who are they?

FRANCESCA.

Berlingerio!

MAN-AT-ARMS

[*starting*].

O, Madonna Francesca!

[*The* ARCHER *remains silent and stares at her blankly, leaning on the catapult.*]

FRANCESCA.

Messer Giovanni
Is at the Mastra yet?

MAN-AT-ARMS.

Not yet, Madonna. We expect him now.

FRANCESCA.

And no one else?

MAN-AT-ARMS.

Yes, Messer Malatesta,
The old man. He himself it was who made
The mixing in the cauldron; and I am here
Since midday with this ladle, stirring it.

FRANCESCA

[*going nearer*].

And no one else?

MAN-AT-ARMS.

And no one else, Madonna.

FRANCESCA.

What are you doing here?

MAN-AT-ARMS.

Making Greek fire,
Distaffs and staves and spouts and lines and pots
And fiery darts, and much
Other caresses for the Parcitadi,
Because we trust to come to blows to-day
And give them from this quarter what shall prove
A good part-payment of their coming hell.

FRANCESCA.

(*Looking wonderingly at the boiling mass in the cauldron*)
Greek fire! Who can escape it? I have never
Seen it before. Tell me, is it not true
That there is nothing known so terrible
In battles for a torture?

MAN-AT-ARMS

This is indeed most terrible; 'tis a secret
That Messer Malatesta
Had from an aged man of Pisa, who
Was with the Christians at the famous taking
Of Damiata.

FRANCESCA.

Tell me, is it true
That it flames in the sea,
Flames in the stream,
Burns up the ships,
Burns down the towers,
Stifles and sickens,
Drains a man's blood in his veins,
Straightway, and makes

Of his flesh and his bones
A little black ashes,
Draws from the anguish
Of man the wild cry of the beast,
That it maddens the horse,
Turns the valiant to stone?
Is it true that it shatters
The rock, and consumes
Iron, and bites
Hard to the heart
Of a breastplate of diamond?

MAN-AT-ARMS.

It bites and eats
All kinds of things that are, living and dead;
Sand only chokes it out,
But also vinegar
Slacks it.

FRANCESCA.

But how do you
Dare, then, to handle it?

MAN-AT-ARMS.

We have the license
Of Beezlebub, that is the prince of devils,
And comes to take the part
Of the Malatesti.

FRANCESCA.

How do you scatter it?

MAN-AT-ARMS.

With tubes and syphons
Of a long range; or at the point of pikes
With distaffs full of flax
We shoot it by the help of our balistas.

See here, Madonna, these are very good
Distaffs; they are
The distaffs of the Guelfs
That without spindle weave the death of men.

[*He takes up a staff prepared for the fire and shows it to* FRANCESCA, *who takes it by the handle and shakes it vehemently.*]

FRANCESCA.

Light one for me.

MAN-AT-ARMS.

The signal is not yet
Given.

FRANCESCA.

I would have you light this one for me.

MAN-AT-ARMS.

Who is to put it out?

FRANCESCA.

O, I must see
The flame that I have never seen as yet.
Light it! Is it not true that when you light it
It darts marvellous colours, like no other
Creature of flight,
Colours of such a mingling that the eye
Cannot endure them,
Of an unspeakable
Variety, innumerable
In fervour and in splendour, that alone
Live in the wandering planets and within
The vials of alchemists:
And in volcanoes full of many metals,
And in the dreams of blind men? Is it true?

MAN-AT-ARMS.

In very deed, Madonna,
It is a beautiful and pleasant thing
To see at night these lighted distaffs fly
And light upon a camp
Of the imperial ragamuffianry;
And that knows well Messer Giovanni, your
Good husband, who takes pleasure to behold it.

FRANCESCA.

Light it, then, man-at-arms! for I must see it.

MAN-AT-ARMS.

'Tis not yet night, nor is the signal given.

FRANCESCA.

Light it! I bid you.
And I will hide myself here in the dark
To see it, by the stairway leading down,
Where it is darker.

MAN-AT-ARMS.

Do you want to burn
The tower with all the archers,
And please the Parcitade folk?

[FRANCESCA *dips the fiery staff into the cauldron, then rapidly lights it with a firebrand.*]

FRANCESCA.

And I
Light it!

[*The violent and many-coloured flame crackles at the point of the pike that she holds in her hand like a torch, fearlessly*].

O, fair flame, conqueror of day!
Ah, how it lives, how it lives vibrating,

The whole staff vibrates with it, and my hand
And my arm vibrate with it, and my heart.
I feel it nearer me
Than if I held it in my palm. Wouldst thou
Devour me, fair flame, wouldst thou make me
thine?
I feel that I am maddening for thee.

(*Her voice rises like a song. The* MAN-AT-ARMS *and the* ARCHER *gaze in astonishment at the flame and the woman, as at some work of sorcery*].

And how it roars!
It roars to seek its prey.
It roars and longs for flight;
And I would fling it up into the clouds.
Come, charge the arbalest.
The sun is dead, and this,
This is the daughter that he had of death.
O I would fling it up into the clouds.
Why do you linger? No, I am not mad,
No, no, poor man-at-arms, who look at me
In wonderment.

[*She laughs.*]

No, but this flame is so
Beautiful, I am drunk with it. I feel
As I were in the flame and it in me.
You, you, do you not see how beautiful,
How beautiful it is? The bitter smoke
Has spoilt your eyes for seeing. If it shines
So gloriously by day, how will it shine
By night?

[*She approaches the trap-door through which the stairs go down into the tower, and lowers*

the burning staff into the darkness.]
A miracle! A miracle!

MAN-AT-ARMS.

Madonna, God preserve us, you will burn
The whole tower down.
Madonna, I pray you!
[*He hastily draws back out of the way of sparks the staves prepared for fire which are lying about*].

FRANCESCA

[*Intent on the light*].
It is a miracle!
It is the joy of the eyes, and the desire
Of splendour and destruction. In the heart
Of silence of this high and lonely mount
Shall I spread forth these gems of frozen fire,
That all the terror of the flame unloose
And bring to birth new ardours in the soul?
Tremendous life of swiftness, mortal beauty!
Swift through the night, swift through the starless night,
Fall in the camp, and seize the armèd man,
Enswathe his sounding armour, glide between
Strong scale and scale, hunt down
The life of veins, and break
The bones asunder, suck the marrow out,
Stifle him, rend him, blind him, but before
The final darkness falls upon his eyes,
Let all the soul within him without hope
Shriek in the splendour that is slaying him.
[*She listens in the direction of the trap-door.*]
Some one is coming up the stairs here. Who
Is coming?

MAN-AT-ARMS

On each floor
We have a hundred men,
Archers and those that work the manganels,
Hidden, and bidden not to move or breathe,
Crammed in together like a sheaf of arrows
Inside a quiver. Perhaps
They saw the flame.

FRANCESCA.

It is one man alone.
His armour clanks upon him.
Who is it coming?

MAN-AT-ARMS.

Lift up the staff, turn it away, Madonna
Francesca, it is surely not an enemy,
Or you are like to burn him in the face.
Perhaps it is Messer Giovanni.

FRANCESCA
[*bending over the opening*].

Who are you?
Who are you?

THE VOICE OF PAOLO.

Paolo!

[FRANCESCA *is silent; she draws back the fiery staff, and the flame, heightened by the sudden movement, lights up the helmet and gorgerin of* PAOLO MALATESTA.

PAOLO *appears, up to the waist, in the opening of the stairs, and turns to* FRANCESCA *who has moved back against the wall, still holding in her hand the iron handle of the staff, which she has lowered to the ground, so that the fire burns perilously near her feet. The* ARCHER *has returned to his post.*]

MAN-AT-ARMS.

You have come just in time, Messer Paolo, just
In time, for all we here
Were like to have been roasted living, we
And all the towers along with us. You see:
Madonna plays
With the Greek fire
As if she held
A lap-dog in a leash.

[FRANCESCA, *pale and leaning against the wall, laughs with a troubled laugh, letting the staff fall from her hand.*]

It is a miracle
That we are not all here in open hell.
You see!

[*He pours sand on the flame in order to extinguish it.* PAOLO *runs up the remaining steps; as he sets foot on the platform of the tower, the* ARCHER *points towards the city, to show where the battle is beginning.*]

ARCHER.

There is tumult in the San Cataldo quarter.
It is breaking out at the Membruto bridge
Over the Patara trench.
And they are fighting at the fullers' mill
Under the gun tower, there, by the Masdogna.

[FRANCESCA *moves away, stepping uncertainly among the arrows and engines heaped around, and goes towards the door by which she had come; she pauses by the pillar that hides her from the eyes of* PAOLO].

MAN-AT-ARMS.

We are still waiting
For the signal, Messer Paolo.
It is almost vespers. What are we to do?

[PAOLO *does not seem to hear, possessed by a single thought, a single anguish. Seeing* FRANCESCA *has gone, he leaves the tower, and goes down one of the little side staircases to rejoin her.*]

PAOLO.

Francesca!

FRANCESCA.

Give the signal. Paolo, give
The signal! Do not fear
For me, Paolo. Let me stay here and hear
The twanging of the bows.
I cannot breathe
When I am shut into my room, among
My trembling women, and I know there is fighting
Out in the city. I would have you give me,
My lord and kinsman, a fair helmet.

PAOLO.

I
Will give you one.

FRANCESCA.

Have you come from Cesena?

PAOLO.

I came to-day.

FRANCESCA.

You stayed
A long while there.

PAOLO.

It took us forty days
With Guido di Monforte in the field
To take Cesena and the castle.

FRANCESCA.

Ah!
You have toiled, I think, too much.
You are a little thinner and a little
Paler, it seems to me.

PAOLO.

There is an Autumn fever
Among the thickets on the Savio.

FRANCESCA.

No,
But you are sick? You tremble. And Orabile,
Has she no medicine for you?

PAOLO.

This fever
Feeds on itself; I ask no medicine,
I seek no herb to heal my sickness, sister.

FRANCESCA.

I had a healing herb
When I was in my father's house, the house
Of my good father, God protect him, God
Protect him! I had a herb, a healing herb,
There in the garden where you came one day
Clothed in a garment that is called, I think,
Fraud, in the gentle world;
But you set foot on it, and saw it not,
And it has never come up any more,
However light your foot may be, my lord
And kinsman. It was dead.

PAOLO.

I saw it not,
I knew not where I was,
Nor who had led my feet into that way,
I did not speak, I did not hear a word,
I had no bounds to cross,
No barriers to break down,
I only saw a rose
That offered itself up to me more living
Than the lips of a fresh wound, and a young song
I heard in the air, and I heard angry blows
Beaten upon a loud and terrible door,
And I heard an angry voice that cried your name
In anger. Only that, nothing but that.
Nor from that way did I come back by will
Of coming back;
Because the ways of death
Are not so secret as that other way,
O sister, if God wills.

FRANCESCA.

I also saw
With my own eyes the dawn,
The dawn that brings with it the morning star,
The nurse of the young heavens,
That had but newly waked to give its milk
When the last dream of sleep
Came to my pillow; and I also saw,
With my own eyes I saw,
With horror and with shame,
About me as it were an impure stream
Of water flung suddenly outraging
A palpitating face

Lifted to drink the light.
This did I see with my own eyes; and this
I shall see always till the night has fallen,
The night that has no dawn,
Brother.

PAOLO.

The shame and horror be on me !
The light that came again
Found me awake.
Peace had forever fled
Out of the soul of Paolo Malatesta;
It has not come again, it will not come
Ever again;
Peace and the soul of Paolo Malatesta
Are enemies from now in life or death.
And all things were as enemies to me
From the hour that you set foot
Upon the threshold, and without escape,
And I turned back and followed with the guide.
Violent deeds
Were the one medicine for my disease,
That night: violent deeds.
And then I killed Tindaro Omodei
And burned his roofs about him.
I gave to the harsh guide another prey.

FRANCESCA.

God shall forgive you this,
God shall forgive you all the blood you shed,
And all the rest,
But not the tears I did not weep, but not
The eyes that were still dry when the dawn came.
I cannot weep now, brother! Another draught
You gave me at the ford

Of the beautiful river, do you remember it?
With your false heart,
Filled full with madness and with treachery,
That was the last, that was the last that quenched
My thirst; and now no water
Can quench my thirst, not any more, my lord.
And then we saw the walls of Rimino,
And then we saw the Galeana gate,
And the sun was going down upon the hills,
And all the horses neighed against the walls,
And then I saw your face,
Silent, between the spears
Of the horsemen. And a wicked thing it was
That you did not let me drift upon the stream,
That would have taken me and laid me down
Softly upon the seashore of Ravenna,
And some one would have found me, and brought me back
To my good father, to my most kind father
That without thought of wrong had given me
To whom he would, yes, without thought of wrong;
God have him in his keeping, give him always
More and more lordship!

PAOLO.

Your rebuke, Francesca,
Is cruel over-much, sweet over-much,
And my heart melts within me, and my sad soul
Is shed before the strangeness of your voice.
My soul is shed before you,
All that is in me have I cast away,
And I will no more stoop to pick it up.
How would you have me die?

FRANCESCA.

Like to the galley-slave
Rowing in the galley that is called Despair,
So would I have you die; and there and then
The memory of that draught
You gave me at the ford
Of the beautiful river,
Before we had come to the water of treachery
And to the walls of fraud, should burn in you
And should consume you. My brother in God,
In the Most High God,
And in Saint John, better it were for you
That you should lose your life than stain your soul.

[*The bells of Santa Colomba are heard. Both shiver as if returning to consciousness.*]

Ah! where are we? Who is it calling us?
Paolo, what hour is that?
What are you doing?

[*The* MAN-AT-ARMS *and the* ARCHER, *busy loading the balistas and cocking the fiery staves, start at the sound.*]

MAN-AT-ARMS.

The signal! It is the signal!
It is the bells of Santa Colomba!

ARCHER.

Fire!
Fire! Long live Malatesta!

[A TROOP OF ARCHERS *hurry shouting up through the trap-door, and through the platform of the tower, and seize weapons and engines.*]

ARCHERS.

Long live Messer Malatesta and the Guelfs! Down with Messer Parcitade and the Ghibellines!

[*On the battlements is a great sheaf of fiery staves, which glows in the dusky air.* PAOLO MALATESTA *takes his helmet from his head and gives it to* FRANCESCA.]

PAOLO.

Here is the helmet that I have to give you.

FRANCESCA.

Paolo!

[PAOLO *rushes upon the tower. His bare head overtops the* MEN-AT-ARMS *as they work.* FRANCESCA, *throwing down the helmet, follows, calling to him through the noise and clamour.*]

PAOLO.

Give me a crossbow!

FRANCESCA.

Paolo! Paolo!

PAOLO.

A bow! A crossbow!

FRANCESCA.

Paolo! Paolo!

[*An* ARCHER *is knocked over by a bolt which takes him in the throat.*]

MAN-AT-ARMS.

Madonna, get you gone, for God's sake; now
They are beginning here to bite the leads.

[*Some* ARCHERS *raise their large painted shields in the way of* FRANCESCA *as she tries to follow* PAOLO.]

ARCHERS.

The Galeana Tower is answering!
Cignatta's men are coming
By the Masdogna!
Long live Messer Malatesta and the Guelfs!
Verrucchio! Verrucchio!

[FRANCESCA *tries to get past the* ARCHERS, *who stop her way.*]

MAN-AT-ARMS.

Madonna,
By any God you worship! Messer Paolo,
Pay a little heed here! Here is Madonna Francesca
Out in the open. It is death here.

[PAOLO, *snatching a crossbow, stands on the rampart, firing furiously, in full view of the enemy, like a madman.*]

FRANCESCA.

Paolo!

[PAOLO *turns at the cry, and sees the woman in the glare of the fires. He snatches a shield from one of the* ARCHERS *and covers her.*]

PAOLO.

Ah, Francesca, go, go! What is this madness?

[*He pushes her toward shelter, holding the shield over her; she gazes at his angry and beautiful face from under the shield.*]

FRANCESCA.

You
Are the madman! You are the madman!

PAOLO.

And was I not to die?

[*He leads her back to shelter and throws down the shield, still holding the crossbow.*]

FRANCESCA.

Not now, not now,
It is not yet the hour.

ARCHERS.

—Malatesta! Malatesta!
—Cignatta's men are there, under the Rubbia!
—This side, this side!

[*They come down by the stairs on the left and set the crossbows to the arrow-slits in the walls. The bells ring in all directions. A distant sound of trumpets is heard.*]

—Verruchio! Down with the Parcitade! Death
To the Ghibelline!
—Long live Messer Malatesta!
Long live the Guelfs!

PAOLO.

This is the hour, if you will see me die,
If you will lift my head out of the dust
With your two hands. What other could I have?
I will not die the death of the galley-slave.

FRANCESCA.

Paolo, steel your heart against your fate,
Be silent as that day
Under the heavy guidance, as that day
Among the spears of the spearmen. And let me not
Stain my own soul for your sake!

PAOLO.

Ay, to play
With fate is what I will,
Is what my false heart wills,
Filled full of madness and of treachery.

[*With an impetuous gesture he draws her towards the fortified window, and puts into her hand the cord that hangs from the portcullis.*]

Throw the portcullis open!
A child's hand opens it,
The mere touch of an innocent hand.

[*He gathers a bundle of arrows and throws them at the feet of* FRANCESCA. *Then he loads the crossbow.*]

FRANCESCA.

Ah, madman!
Madman! And do you think
My hand will tremble? Do you think to tempt
My soul after this fashion? I am ready
For any mortal game men play with fate,
Knowing I shall not lose,
Seeing that all is lost.
But you now stand
Upon tremendous limits, where God help you!
I open for you. See!
Look straight before you,
And take the sign, if you would not have me laugh.

[*She pulls the portcullis open with the cord, and through the opening is seen the open sea, shining under the last rays of light.*]

The sea! The sea!

[PAOLO *aims the crossbow and fires.*]

PAOLO.

A good stroke! It is gone
Through neck and neckpiece.
That's my good forerunner
In the land of darkness!

[FRANCESCA *lowers the portcullis, and the return arrow is heard against it.* PAOLO *reloads the crossbow.*]

ARCHERS

[*On the tower*].

—Victory!
Victory! Death, death to the Parcitadi!
Long live Messer Malatesta and the Guelfs!
—Victory! Victory! the Ghibelline is broken
At the Patara bridge.
—The fuller's mill is empty!
—Messer Giovanni galloping with the spears
At the Gattolo gate! Cignatta scampering!
—Be careful not to wound
Our own folk in the fray!
—Victory to Malatesta!

FRANCESCA

[*In great emotion*].

I have seen the sea,
The eternal sea,
The witness of the Lord,
And on the sea a sail
That the Lord set to be a sign of saving.
Paolo, brother in God,
I make a vow
If the Lord of mercy
Have you in keeping!

PAOLO.

Raise the portcullis up!

FRANCESCA

I will not let it down again. This hazard
Shall be God's judgment, this judgment of the
arrow.
Man is deceit, but God is very truth.
Brother in God, the stain of fraud you have
Upon your soul,
Let it be pardoned to you with all love,
And let the judgment of God
Make proof of you
Now by the arrow
That it touch you not;
Or it were better
That you give your life,
And I with you.

[*Holding the tightened cord in her hand she kneels and prays, with her wide-open eyes fixed on* PAOLO'S *unarmed head. Through the raised portcullis can be seen the shining sea.* PAOLO *loads and fires the crossbow without a pause. From time to time Ghibelline missiles enter by the window and strike on the opposite wall or fall on the pavement without wounding him. The cruel suspense convulses the face of the woman in prayer. The syllables hardly form themselves on her parted lips.*]

Our Father which art in heaven,
Hallowed be thy name,
Thy Kingdom come,
Thy will be done in earth

As it is in heaven.
Father, give us this day
Our daily bread.

[PAOLA, *having failed in several shots, takes aim more carefully, as if for a master-stroke. He fires; a clamour is heard among the enemy.*]

PAOLO

[*With fierce delight*].

Ah, Ugolino, I have found you out!

FRANCESCA.

And forgive us our debts, as we
Forgive our debtors.
And lead us not
Into temptation,
But deliver us from evil.
So be it, Amen.

[*Meanwhile there is great rejoicing among the* ARCHERS *on the tower. Some carry the killed and wounded down through the trap-door.*]

ARCHERS.

—Victory to Malatesta!
—Death to the Parcitadi and the Ghibellines!
Montagna's men are flying
By the San Cataldo gate.—See, see, the fire
Is spreading. There's a powder-barrel burst
Over the house of Accarisio. See,
The fire is spreading! —Victory! Malatesta!
—Ah, Messer Ugolino
Cignatta has fallen from his horse. He is dead!

—A bolt from a crossbow took him in the mouth.
Who was it killed him? Was it Bartolo
Gambitta?
—Who, who killed him? One of ours?
A splendid stroke!
—Deserves a hundred lire,
A thousand golden crowns!—Victory! Victory!

[*A shaft grazes the head of* PAOLO MALATESTA, *passing through his hair.* FRANCESCA *utters a cry, letting go the cord; starting to her feet, she takes his head in her hands, feeling for the wound. A mortal pallor overspreads his face at the touch. The crossbow falls at his feet.*]

FRANCESCA.

Paolo! Paolo!

[*She looks at her hands to see if they are stained with blood. They are white. She again searches anxiously.*]

O, what is this? Oh, God!
Paolo! Paolo! You are not bleeding, and you have
No single drop of blood upon your head,
Yet you look deathly. Paolo!

PAOLO

[*In a choking voice*].

I am not dying,
Francesca. Iron has not touched me.

FRANCESCA.

Saved!
O saved and pure! Cleansed utterly of fraud!
Give thanks to God! Kneel, brother!

PAOLO.

But your hands
Have touched me, and the soul
Has fainted in my heart, and icy cold
Takes hold on all my veins, and no more strength
Is in me now to live;
But of this other life
That comes to meet me—

FRANCESCA.

Kneel, kneel, on your life!

PAOLO.

Ah! an unspeakable fear takes hold on me,
And a scorn deeper even than the fear—

FRANCESCA.

Kneel! Kneel!

PAOLO.

Since I have lived
With such an infinite force,
Fighting apart, yet ever on the lonely
Height of your prayer,
And in the fiery solitude of your eyes—

FRANCESCA.

Kneel! Kneel! Give thanks to God!
I will not lose you now over again!

PAOLO.

Fighting apart, and slaying
Men—

FRANCESCA.

You are pardoned now,
And you are cleansed, and yet you will be lost!

PAOLO.

And all my courage drawn
Vehemently about my angry heart,

And all within me now
The power of my most evil love sealed up.

FRANCESCA.

Lost! Lost! Say you are mad,
Say, on your life, that you are mad, and say
That your most wretched soul
Has heard no word of all your mouth has said!
By the arrow that passed by
And struck you not,
By the death that touched you with its finger-tip
And took you not,
Say that your life shall never, never speak
Those words again!

ARCHERS.

Long live Messer Giovanni Malatesta!

[GIOVANNI MALATESTA *comes up by the stairs of the Mastra Tower, armed from head to foot, and holding a Sardinian rod in his hand. He limps up the stairs, and, when he has reached the top, raises his terrible spear, while his harsh voice cuts through the clamour.*]

GIANCIOTTO.

By God, you craven creatures,
You cut-throat spawn,
I am well minded
To pitch you all headlong into the Ausa,
Like carrion that you are.

FRANCESCA.

Your brother!

[PAOLO *picks up the crossbow*].

GIANCIOTTO.

You are more ready
To cry rejoicings
Than to belabour this tough Ghibelline hide.
How should you work your crossbows without sinews?
Had I not come to aid you with my horse,
Cignatta would have battered down your gates;
God break the arms of all of you for cowards!

ARCHERS.

—We had used almost all our stock of arrows.
—The Astrologer was late in signalling.
—We have silenced them on the Galassa tower.
—We have piled up a heap on the Masdogna.

GIANCIOTTO.

Poor fire, by God! There are not many houses
To be seen burning. Badly thrown, your fire.

ARCHERS.

—The house of Accarisio is still burning.
—And the good Cignatta, who unhorsed him then?
—It was one of us that slit his windpipe for him?

GIANCIOTTO.

Which one of you was standing at the window?

ARCHERS.

—Was not this one here something of the cut?
A thousand golden crowns to the company!

GIANCIOTTO.

Who was it at the window?

ARCHERS.

—We have been slaving on an empty stomach.
—We are dead with hunger and with thirst.
—Long live
Messer Gianciotto the never-satisfied!

[PAOLO *picks up his helmet, puts it on and goes towards the tower.* FRANCESCA *goes towards the door by which she had entered, opens it and calls.*]

FRANCESCA.

O Smaragdi! Smaragdi!

GIANCIOTTO

[*To the* ARCHERS].

Be silent there. Your tongues dry up in you!
No talking while you work: I like you silent.
But come now, there is a great cask to hurl;
I will teach you the right way of it; and I will send it
To the old Parcitade for leave-taking
In my good father's name. Here, Berlingerio,
Where is my brother Paolo?
Did he not come up here?

[*The* SLAVE *appears at the door; then, after an order from her mistress, disappears.* FRANCESCA *remains standing on the threshold.*]

PAOLO.

Here. I am here, Gianciotto. It was I
Who shot out of the window. The dumb thing
Struck through the throat of one whose mouth was open
To jest at you.

[*There is a murmur among the* ARCHERS.]

GIANCIOTTO.

Brother, much thanks for this.

[*He turns to the* MEN-AT-ARMS].

So sure a shot must needs
Come from a Malatesta,
My braggart bowmen.

[*The* SLAVE *reappears with a jar and a cup.* FRANCESCA *comes forward.* GIANCIOTTO *comes down towards his brother.*]

Paolo, I bring you news,
Good news.

[*He sees his wife. His voice changes to a gentler tone.*]

Francesca!

FRANCESCA.

All hail, my lord; you bring the victory.

[*He goes up to her and embraces her.*]

GIANCIOTTO.

Dear lady, why are you in such a place.

[*She draws back from the embrace.*]

FRANCESCA.

You have blood upon your armour.

GIANCIOTTO.

Have I painted you?

FRANCESCA.

You are all over dust.

GIANCIOTTO.

Lady, the dust
Is bread to me.

FRANCESCA.

You are not wounded?

GIANCIOTTO.

Wounds?

I feel none.

FRANCESCA.

But you must be thirsty.

GIANCIOTTO.

Yes,

I am very thirsty.

FRANCESCA.

Samaragdi, bring the wine.

[*The* SLAVE *comes forward with the jar and the cup.*]

GIANCIOTTO

[*With delighted surprise*].

What my dear lady, you have taken thought
I might be thirsty? Why, you must have set
Your slave to watch for me, that you should know
My coming to the minute.

[FRANCESCA *pours out the wine and hands the cup to her husband.* PAOLO *stands aside in silence, watching the men who are preparing the fiery cask.*]

FRANCESCA.

Drink, it is wine of Scios.

GIANCIOTTO.

Drink first, I pray you.

A draught.

FRANCESCA.

I have not poisoned it, my lord.

GIANCIOTTO.

You laugh at me. Not for suspicion's sake,
But for the favour, for the favour of it,

Francesca, my true wife.
I have no fear of treachery from you.
My horse has not yet stumbled under me.
Drink, lady.
[FRANCESCA *touches the cup with her lips.*]
It is sweet,
After the fight, to see your face again,
To take a strong wine from your hands, and drink it
Down at a draught.
[*He empties the cup.*]
So. Why this warms my heart.
And Paolo? Where is Paolo?
Why has he not a word for you? He comes
Back from Cesena, and not
A word of welcome has my kinsman from you.
Paolo, come here. Are you not thirsty? Leave
Greek fire for Greek wine. Then
We will burn up the Parcitadi living!
Lady, pour out for him a cup brimful
And drink with him a draught, to do him honour;
And welcome him, welcome the perfect archer.

FRANCESCA.

I have already greeted him.

GIANCIOTTO.

But when?

FRANCESCA.

When he was shooting.

PAOLO.

Do you know, Gianciotto,
I came up on the tower

And found her in the act of making trial
With Berlingerio of a fiery dart?

GIANCIOTTO.

Is that the truth?

PAOLO.

She played
With lighted fire, and the poor man-at-arms
Was crying out for fear the tower should burn,
And she the while was laughing. I heard her laugh,
While the fire lay as gentle at her feet
As a greyhound in leash.

GIANCIOTTO.

Is that the truth,
Francesca?

FRANCESCA.

I was weary of my rooms
And of my whimpering women. And of a truth
I had rather look, my lord, on open war
Than feed fear closeted.

GIANCIOTTO.

Daughter of Guido,
Your father's seal is on you. May God make you
Fruitful to me, that you may give me many
And many a lion's cub!

[FRANCESCA *knits her brow.*]

Paolo, you have not drunk!
Drink, you are pale, Pour out a cup for him,
My woman warrior, full, and drink a draught.
He shot a splendid bolt.

PAOLO.

Do you know, Gianciotto,
Who lifted up the window while I shot?
She! In her hand she held the little cord
That lifts it, like the children of our soldiers;
And steady was her hand and firm her eye.

GIANCIOTTO.

Why, come then, come, my lady, and make war
Among the castles! I will make for you
A breastplate of fine gold, and you shall go
Riding with sword and spear,
Like the brave Countess Aldruda di Bertinoro,
When she went out to fight with Marchesella
Against the Councillor of Magonza. Ah!
You have been apart from me too long, dear lady.
Now with that dark band underneath your chin
And round your neck, you seem to wear a gorget:
It gives you a wild sort of grace. True, eh,
Paozzo? But you have not yet drunk! Drink, now.
Drink, you are pale. You have worked well. This night
We shall not sleep, two in our beds. So, lady,
Pour out the wine.

FRANCESCA.

See, I am pouring it.

GIANCIOTTO.

It is almost dark here; one can hardly see;
You might have spilt it.

FRANCESCA.

Drink, my lord and kinsman,
Out of the cup in which your brother drank.
God give you both good fortune,
Each as the other, and alike to me!

[PAOLO *drinks, looking straight into* FRANCESCA'S *eyes.*]

GIANCIOTTO.

Good fortune, Paolo,
I had begun to tell you, and I stopped;
I have happy tidings for you. In the hour
Of victory there came to our good father
Envoys from Florence, saying you are elected
The Captain of the People and the Commune
Of Florence.

PAOLO.

Envoys came!

GIANCIOTTO.

Why, yes. You are sorry?

PAOLO.

No, I will go.

[FRANCESCA *turns her face to the shadow and moves a few steps nearer the tower. The* SLAVE *retires to one side and stands motionless.*]

GIANCIOTTO.

You must go within three days.
You will have time to go to Ghiaggiolo
To your Orabile, who is used by now
To being a widow. And from there you will go
To the city of gay living that has thriven
Under the guidance of the joyous friars,
Full of fat merchants, and of merry-makers,

And gentry of the Court, and there the tables
Are spread both night and morning, and they dance there
And sing there, and you can sport to heart's content.

[*His face clouds over and he becomes bitter again.*]

We will stay here and set the trap for wolves
And slit the throats of lambkins. Iron shall knock
On iron for the pleasure of our ears,
Sardinian rod and hatchet of Orezzo
On bolt with rounded edge, morning and night
And night and morning. Here then we will wait
Till in some escalade another stone
Fracture another knee. And then, why, then,
Giovanni, the old Lamester, Gianni Ciotto,
Shall have himself tied tightly on the back
Of a stallion with the staggers, and so slung
Neck and crop ravaging down the ways of hell.

[FRANCESCA *moves restlessly to and fro in the shadow, Through the archway is seen the evening sky reddened by the flames*].

PAOLO.

Giovanni, are you angry with me?

GIANCIOTTO.

No,
Did you not split the tongue of him who cried
His jests against me? "At him! At him! Ha!
The Lamester with the lovely wife!" cried out
Ugolino as he rode. His voice was loud:

Did it reach you at the window? I was there,
Eye upon eye, and stirrup against stirrup,
When your good shaft went straight
Into his snarling mouth,
And through, and out the back way of the head.
And yet you might have missed.
I felt the feathers of the arrow-shaft
Whistle against my face. You might have missed.

PAOLO.

But since I did not miss, why think of it?

GIANCIOTTO.

It is your way to run these sorts of risks.
At Florence be more cautious. You are going
To a hard post. Have sharp and rapid sight
But also prudent hand.

PAOLO.

Since you advise me,
Does it not seem to you, brother, as if
'Twere wiser let it go? We shall have need
Of all our forces here. The year is turnina
Not over fortunately for the Guelfs,
Since the defeat of that Giovanni d'Appia
And the rebellion since in Sicily,
In favour of the Angevins.

GIANCIOTTO.

We must needs
Accept, and that without delay. You now
Shall be the keeper of the peace where once
Our mighty father was the Governor
Under King Charles, in the one great Guelf city

That prospers still. And so beyond the bounds
Of our Romagna shall the name of us
Sound high and spread abroad; and each of us
Shall follow where his rising star leads on.
I go my way, my sword has eyes for me;
My horse has not yet stumbled under me.

[*While he speaks,* MALATESTINO *is brought, wounded, down the stairs of the tower, between lighted torches, like a corpse. The shadow grows darker*].

FRANCESCA

[*From the back*].

O, what is this? Horror! Do you not see
Malatestino, there, Malatestino,
The soldiers carrying him in their arms
Between the torches? They have killed his father!

She runs towards the MEN, *who are coming down the side stairs, and passing through the midst of the archers, who leave off their work and make way in silence.* GIANCIOTTO *and* PAOLO *run forward.* ODDO DALLE CAMINATE *and* FOSCOLO D'OLNANO *are carrying the bleeding* YOUTH. FOUR ARCHERS *with long quivers accompany them with torches.*

FRANCESCA

[*Bending over the* YOUTH].

Malatestino! O God,
His eye is black with blood,
His eye is cut and torn. How have they killed him?

O, has his father seen it? Does he know?

[GIANCIOTTO *feels over his body and listens to his heart.*]

GIANCIOTTO.

Francesca, no, he is not dead! He breathes,
His heart is beating still. Do you not see?
He is coming to. The blow has struck him senseless;
But he is coming to.
The life is sound in him; he has good teeth
To keep it back from going. Courage, now!
Set him down gently here, here on this heap
Of ropes.

[*As the* BEARERS *are setting him down, the* YOUTH *begins to revive.*]

Oddo, how was it?

ODDO.

From a stone
While they were scaling the Galassa tower.

FOSCOLO.

All by himself he had made prisoner
Montagna Parcitade,
And bound him with his sword-belt, and led him back
To Messer Malatesta; and returned
To take the Tower.

ODDO.

Just as he was, without
A visor to his helmet, heedlessly:
You know how hot he is!

FOSCOLO.

And he was angry

Because his father would not suffer him
To cut the prisoner's throat.

[FRANCESCA *pours a few drops of wine between the lips of the* YOUTH. PAOLO *follows every movement greedily with his eyes.*]

GIANCIOTTO

[*Looking at the wound*].

A stone out of the hand; not from a sling.
Come, it is nothing.
Lean as he is, he needs
Crow-bar and catapult to put him under.
This is a heart of metal, a tough liver.
He bears the sign of God now, as I do,
In warfare. He shall be
Named, from henceforth, as I am, by his scar.

[*He kisses him on the forehead.*]

Malatestino!

[*The* YOUTH *shakes himself and recovers consciousness.*]

Drink, Malatestino!

[*He drinks some of the wine, which* FRANCESCA *puts to his lips. Then he shakes his head, and is about to raise to his wounded left eye the hand still wearing its gauntlet.* FRANCESCA *prevents him.*]

MALATESTINO.

[*As if suddenly awaking, with violence*].

He will escape, I say. He is not safe
In prison. I tell you he will find a way
To escape presently. Father, give me leave
To cut his throat! I took him for you! Father,

Dear Father, let me kill him. I am sure
He will find a way to escape presently.
He is an evil one. Well, you then, give him
One hammer-stroke upon the head; one blow,
And he will turn upon himself three times.

FRANCESCO.

Malatestino, what do you see? You are raving,
What do you see, Malatestino?

ODDO.

Still
He is raging at Montagna.

GIANCIOTTO.

Malatestino, do you not know me? See,
You are on the Mastra Tower.
Montagna is in good clutches. Be assured
He will not run away from you.

MALATESTINO.

Giovanni,
Where am I? O Francesca, and you too?
[*He again raises his hand to his eye.*]
What is the matter with my eye?

GIANCIOTTO.

A stone
That caught you in it.

FRANCESCA.

Are you suffering much?
[*The* YOUTH *rises to his feet and shakes his head.*]

MALATESTINO.

The stone-throw of a Ghibelline camp-follower
To make me suffer?
Come, come, there's no use now

No time to weave new linen with old thread.
Put on a bandage, quick,
Give me to drink, and then
To horse, to horse!

[FRANCESCA *takes off the band that surrounds her chin and throat.*]

GIANCIOTTO.

Can you see?

MALATESTINO.

One's enough for me.

GIANCIOTTO.

Try now
If the left one is lost.

[*He takes a torch from one of the* ARCHERS.]

Close your right eye. Francesca,
Put your hand over it. He has his gauntlet.

[*She closes his eyelid with her fingers.* GIANCIOTTO *puts the torch before his face.*]

Look! Do you see this torch?

MALATESTINO.

No.

GIANCIOTTO.

Not a glimmer?

MALATESTINO.

No, no!

[*He takes* FRANCESCA'S *wrist and pushes it away.*]

But I can see with one.

ARCHER

[*Excited by the* YOUTH'S *courage*].

Long live
Messer Malatestino! Malatesta!

MALATESTINO.

To horse, to horse!
Giovanni, though the day is won, yet, yet,
Is not old Parcitade living still,
And waiting reinforcements? We must not
Be blinded. Oddo, Foscolo, the best
Is still to have.

GIANCIOTTO

[*turning to the* ARCHERS].

The cask! is the cask ready?

[*He goes towards the tower, to direct the operations of the catapult.*]

ODDO.

You will fall half-way there.

FRANCESCA.

Stay, Malatestino,
Do not go back into the fight! Stay here,
And I will bathe and heal you. Run, Smaragdi,
Prepare the water and the linen; send
For Maestro Almodoro.

MALATESTINO.

No, kinswoman,
Put on a bandage, quick,
And let me go. I will come back again
To find the doctor: bid the doctor wait.
I feel no pain at all.
But bandage me, I beg of you, kinswoman,
With the band that you have taken off your face.

FRANCESCA.

I will do the best I can for you, God knows,

But it will not be well done.

[*She binds up his eye. He observes* PAOLO, *who has not taken his eyes off* FRANCESCA.]

MALATESTINO.

O, Paozzo,
What are you doing there? dreaming?

FRANCESCA.

'Twill not
Be well done.

MALALESTINO.

You have been elected Captain
Of the People at Florence. When I haled Montagna
Up to our father, bound, I saw the envoys,
The Guelfs of the Red Lily,
Who were with him then.

[*A guttural cry is heard as the* MEN *raise the cask upon the catapult. Above the battlements the glow of the fire spreads over the sky. The bells ring in all directions. Trumpets are heard.*]

They have shut up Montagna
In the sea prison. He will get away.
I begged my father, I begged him, on my knees,
To let me finish.
The envoys smiled. My father would not let me,
Because of them, I know,
To seem magnanimous. Another night
Montagna must not spend here. Will you help me?
Come to the prison! Have you done, kinswoman?
But do not tremble.

FRANCESCA

[*Tying the knot*].

Yes, yes, but it is not well done. Your forehead
Is burning. You are feverish. Do not go,
Malatestino. Listen to me. Stay,
For God's sake!

GIANCIOTTO

[*On the tower*].

Heave it! Let it go!

[*The noise of the catapult is heard as it discharges the cask with its lighted fuses*]

ARCHER.

Long life
To Malatesta! Long life to the Guelfs!
Death to the Ghibellines and Parcitade!

MALATESTINO

[*turning and running forward*].

To horse! to horse! to horse!

[ODDO, FOSCOLO, *and the* ARCHERS *with their torches follow him.*]

[*The stage darkens. The reflection of the fire reddens the shadow in which* PAOLO *and* FRANCESCA *remain alone.*]

PAOLO.

Farewell, Francesca.

[*As he approaches her, she draws back with terror.*]

GIANCIOTTO

[*From the tower*].

Paolo! Paolo!

FRANCESCA.

Brother, farewell! Brother!

[PAOLO *goes towards the Tower, from which the fiery staves are again being thrown.* FRANCESCA, *left alone in the shadow, makes the sign of the cross and falls on her knees, bowing herself to the ground. At the back a still brighter illumination lights up the sky.*]

ARCHER.

Fire! fire! Death to the Ghibellines! Fire! Death
To Parcitade and the Ghibellines!
Long live the Guelfs and long live Malatesta!

[*The fiery shafts are let fly through the battlements. The bells ring in all directions. The trumpets sound in the midst of cries rising from the streets of the burning and blood-stained city.*]

ACT III.

A room painted in fresco, elegantly divided into panels, portraying stories out of the romance of Tristan, between birds, beasts, flowers, and fruits. Under the moulding, around the walls, runs a frieze in the form of festoons, on which are written some words from a love-song:

"Meglio m'è dormire gaudendo
C'avere penzieri veghiando."

On the right is a beautiful alcove hidden by rich curtains; on the left a doorway covered by a heavy hanging; at the back a long window with many panes, divided by little columns, looking out on the Adriatic; a pot of basil is on the window-sill. Near the door, raised two feet above the floor, is a musicians' gallery, with compartments decorated with open carvings. Near the window is a reading desk, on which is open "The History of Launcelot of the Lake," composed of large illuminated pages, firmly bound together by thin boards covered in crimson velvet. Besides it is a couch, a sort of long chair without back or arms, with many cushions of samite, almost on the level of the window-sill, on which any one leaning back can see over the whole sea-shore of Rimini. A chamber organ of small size, with chest, pipes, keys, bellows, and registers finely worked, stands in the corner, a lute and a viol beside it. On a small table is a silver mirror, amongst scent-bottles, glasses, purses, girdles, and other trinkets. Large iron candlesticks stand beside the alcove and the musicians' gallery. Footstools are scattered about, and in the midst of the floor is seen the bolt of a trap-door, through which a passage leads to the lower rooms.

[FRANCESCA *is reading in the book. The* WOMEN, *seated on the footstools in a circle, embroidering the border of a coverlet, listen to the story; each of them has a little phial of seed pearls and gold threads hanging from her girdle. The March sunlight beats on the crimson taffeta, and sheds a diffused light on the faces bent over the needlework. The* SLAVE *is near the window-sill, gazing into the sky.*]

FRANCESCA

[*reading*].

" Thereat Galeotto comes to her and says :
'Lady, have pity on him, for God's sake,
And do for me as I would do for you,
If you should ask it of me.' 'What is this
That I should pity ?' 'Lady, you well know
How much he loves you, and has done for you,
More than knight ever did for any lady.'
'In truth he has done more for me than I
Can ever do for him again, and he
Could ask of me nothing I would not do ;
But he asks nothing of me, and he has

So deep a sadness, that I marvel at it."
And Galeotto says: 'Lady, have pity.'
'That will I have,' says she, 'and even such
As you would have me; but he asks of me
Nothing. . .'"

[*The* WOMEN *laugh.* FRANCESCA *throws herself back on the cushions, troubled and enervated.*]

GARSENDA.

Madonna,
How ever could a knight, and Launcelot,
Have been so shamefaced?

ALDA.

All the while the queen,
The poor queen, only longing she might give
Her lover what he would not ask of her!

BIANCOFIORE.

She should have said to him: "Most worthy knight,
Your sadness will avail you not a mite."

ALTICHIARA.

Guenevere did but jest with him, and chose
To wait her time; but nothing in the world
Was in her mind more than a speedy bed.

ADONELLA.

And Galeotto, though indeed he was
A noble prince, knew well enough the art
That is called—

FRANCESCA.

Adonella, hush! I tire

Of listening to your chattering so long.
Smaragdi, tell me, is the falcon back?

SLAVE.

No, lady; he has lost his way.

FRANCESCA.

Do you hear
His little golden bell?

SLAVE.

I cannot hear it.
My eyes are good, and yet I cannot see him.
He has flown too high.

[FRANCESCA *turns to the window and gazes out.*]

ALDA.

He will be lost, Madonna.
It was not well to let him out of leash.
He was a little haughty.

GARSENDA.

He was one
They call the Ventimillia breed, brave birds;
This one had thirteen feathers in his tail.

ALTICHIARA.

Their home is on an island;
He will have flown back to his island home.

BIANCOFIORE.

He followed cranes, was good at catching them;
And Simonetto begs of you, Madonna,
That he may have a crane, to make two fifes
Of the two leg-bones, and he says they sound
Sweetly as might be.

GARSENDA.

No,
He is not coming back; he was too proud;
Ah, like the one who gave him to you, Messer
Malatestino, I would say: may he
Not hear me! If you had but rubbed his beak,
At dead of night,
With horse's belly-grease,
He would have come to love you so, Madonna,
He never would have flown out of your hand.

[*The* WOMEN *burst out laughing.*]

ADONELLA.

Now listen to the learned doctoress!

ALTICHIARA.

At dead of night with horse's belly-grease!

GARSENDA.

Why, yes, I have read the book that Danchi wrote,
The first and best master of falconry;
It gives you all the rules.

FRANCESCA.

Go, Adonella,
Run to the falconer, tell him what has happened,
And bid him go with his decoy, and call
And search all over. He has flown, perhaps,
Up to some tower, and perched there. Bid him go
And search all over.

[ADONELLA *drops her needle and hurries out.*]

ALTICHIARA.

He has fled away,
Madonna, after the first swallows.

ALDA.

See,
The blood of all the swallows
Is raining on the sea.

BIANCOFIORE

[*singing*].
"Fresh in the Calends of March,
O swallows, coming home,
Fresh from the quiet lands beyond the sea."

FRANCESCA.

O, yes, yes, Biancofiore!
Some music, give me music!
Sing over a low song
In the minor key!
Leave off your sewing, go
And bring me music.
[*The* WOMEN *rise quickly and fold up the taffeta.*]
Look
For Simonetto, Biancofiore.

BIANCOFIORE.

Yes,
Madonna.

FRANCESCA.

And you, Alda, look for Bordo
And Signorello and Rosso,
And bid them come and bring the instruments
And bring the tablature
For making music in the room here.

ALDA.

Yes,
Madonna.

FRANCESCA.

Altichiara, if you see
The doctor, send him to me.

ALTICHIARA.

Yes, Madonna.

FRANCESCA.

And you, Garsenda, if you come across
The merchant who is here from Florence bid him
Come hither.

GARSENDA.

Yes, Madonna, I will seek him.

FRANCESCA.

Bring me a garland of March violets·
To-day 'tis the March calends.

BIANCOFIORE.

Madonna, you shall have one, and a fair one.

[*All go out.*]

[FRANCESCA *turns to the* SLAVE, *who is still gazing into the sky*].

FRANCESCA.

O Smaragdi, he is not coming back?

SLAVE.

He is not coming back.
The falconer will bring him back again.
Do not be troubled.

FRANCESCA.

But I am troubled, yes; Malatestino

Will be enraged with me, because I have kept
His gifts so ill. He tells me that he gave me
The king of falcons. I have lost it.

SLAVE.

Wild
And thankless and unkind, if so it flies
From the face of man.

[FRANCESCA *is silent for a few instants.*]

FRANCESCA.

I am afraid of him.

SLAVE.

Afraid of whom, lady?

FRANCESCA.

I am afraid
Of Malatestino.

SLAVE.

Is it his blind eye
That frightens you?

FRANCESCA.

No, no, the other one,
The one he sees with: it is terrible.

SLAVE.

Let him not see you, lady.

FRANCESCA.

Ah, Smaragdi, what was the wine you brought
That night, upon the Mastra tower, when all
The city was in arms? Was it bewitched?

SLAVE.

Lady, what are you saying?

FRANCESCA.

It is as if you brought me a drugged wine;

The poison is taking hold
Upon the veins of her that drank of it,
And all my fate grows cruel to me again.

SLAVE.

What is this sadness, lady?
Although the falcon has not yet come back,
He has come back to you,
Lady, who is the sun that your soul loves.

FRANCESCA

[*turning pale, and speaking with repressed anger*].

Unhappy woman!
How do you dare to speak it? Treachery
Even in you? Accursed be the hour
In which you brought him to me, and his fraud
With him! Was it not you
Who made the way that leads me to my death?
Three cups of bitterness I do not leave you;
It is you that set them down before me, you
That brim them up each day, without a tear.

[*The* SLAVE *flings herself on the ground.*]

SLAVE.

Tread on me, tread on me! Between two stones
Crush in my head!

FRANCESCA

[*More calmly*].

Rise up,
It is no fault of yours, my poor Smaragdi,
It is no fault of yours.
Suddenly like a spirit of my heart
You ran to meet my joy! On your eyes too
There was a veil; and veiled by the same fate

Was the iniquity of my father. We,
All of us, were made powerless and unpitying,
Wretched and ignorant,
Upon the bank of a river,
Unblamable all of us,
Upon the bank of a loud rushing river.
I crossed it, I alone,
I had no thought of you;
I found myself upon the other side.
And we are thrust apart,
Ah me, and never to be one again.
And I now say to you:
I cannot. And you say:
Cross and come back.
And I: I do not know.

[*She gives to the last words almost the cadence of a melody; then she laughs a dry and bitter laugh, which seems as if torn out of her. But the sound of her own laughter frightens her. The* SLAVE *stands trembling.*]

O my poor reason, rule
Still, do not turn away!
What is this demon that has hold on me?
The enemy was laughing in my heart:
Did you not hear him?
I cannot pray now, I can pray no longer.

SLAVE
[*In a low voice*].

Shall I not call him?

FRANCESCA
[*Starting*].

Who?

[*She looks about her anxiously: her eye turns to the motionless curtain over the door. Her craving overcomes her, her voice sounds hoarse.*]

Smaragdi, did you see Messer Giovanni
Take horse?

SLAVE.

Yes, lady, with the old man too,
With Messer Malatesta, the old man.
They are going surely to an act of peace
With the Lord Bishop. They are riding now
By Sant' Arcangelo

FRANCESCA

[*darkly*].

You watch, Smaragdi; you see all, hear all,
Know all; well, be so always.

SLAVE.

Doubt me not,
Lady. Sleep safe and sound. Could I but give you
Joy, as the stone whose name I bear could give you!

FRANCESCA.

And do you know where Malatestino is?

SLAVE.

At Roncofreddo, sent there by his father
With thirty horse.

FRANCESCA.

I am afraid of him.
Keep him away from me.

SLAVE.

But why so, lady?
When he was sick, did you not care for him,
Day and night, like a sister?

FRANCESCA.

O, that name
Is like a poison here. Samaritana,
Where are you? and the stream of your young freshness,
Where does it run, that now can never slake
My thirst when I am nigh to perishing?
I see about me, in the shadow about me,
Eyes, savage eyes, that spy on me, the eyes
Of wild beasts only waiting to take hold
And fight over their prey;
And they are all veined with the selfsame blood,
They are all brothers;
One mother gave them birth. Ah me! what sad
Sorcery have I suffered? Who has set
Thus, thus, upon the threshold of my life
This mortal sin? You, creature of the earth,
Who dig about the roots of poisonous flowers,
Say, where was this unnatural evil born?
It is from you I know
The old hard song:
"If three I find, three I take!" Now the demon
Has taken them all together, three has taken,
And me with them.

SLAVE.

Call not upon the enemy!

Be it forgiven to you, body and soul!
You are deceived in this.
The shadow is a glass to you, and therein
You see your own eyes burn.
Call not upon your head
Some evil fortune! May the Lord God watch
Over you as your slave will surely watch!

FRANCESCA.

There is no escape, Smaragdi. You have said it:
The shadow is a glass to me; and God
Lets me be lost. What days
And nights I spent alone by the bedside
Of the sick man, that I might purge myself
Of evil thoughts that faded, faded out.
I touched the horrible wound,
Praying; I washed away
That evil foulness with my prayers. And then
My soul, amid that horror, seemed to see
Grace and salvation; then it was I found
The beast desire that wakened in the veins
Of that too violent life. Do you understand?
The gaping wound under the forehead closed
And another opened, far more horrible,
Within the breast. And thoughts
That had faded out, my old despairing thoughts,
Seemed to infect me with a blacker venom,
More cruelly; and my flesh
Upon my sorrow like a covering
Intolerable;
And exiled from the world
All the sweet things of springtide and of sleep;

And the very face of love
Turned into stone, and turned
To a terror; only hatred and desire,
Bewildered in the darkness of the world,
And reeling blindly in their work of death,
Like drunken slaughterers,
That, full of wine
And fury, slay each other witlessly.

SLAVE

[*in a low voice*].

Do not despair! Listen, listen! I know
A spell to cast on him who makes you fear;
I know a drink that drives these thoughts away
And cures remembrance. You must give it him
With the left hand
When he dismounts wearied and hungering.
I will teach you how to say the spell.

FRANCESCA.

Smaragdi,
If it avails at all, give it to me,
And let me drink it, and be free again.
But there is no escape. Will you interpret
The dream I always dream,
Night after night?

SLAVE.

Lady, tell me the dream;
I will interpret it.

FRANCESCA.

Night after night I see the savage hunt
Nastagio degli Onesti saw one day

In the pine-wood of Ravenna, as I heard
Bannino tell the story when we went
Down to the shore at Chiassi. In my dream
I see it as it was in very truth.
A naked woman, through the depth of the wood,
Dishevelled, torn by branches and by thorns,
Weeping and crying for mercy,
Runs, followed by two mastiffs at her heels
That bite her cruelly when they overtake her;
See, and behind her through the depth of the wood,
Mounted on a black charger,
A dark knight, strong and angry in the face,
Sword in hand, threatening her
With a swift death in terrifying words.
Then the dogs, taking hold
Of the woman's naked side,
Stop her; and the fierce knight, coming abreast,
Dismounts from off his horse,
And with his sword in hand
Runs at the woman so,
And she, upon her knees, pinned to the earth
By the two mastiffs, cries to him for mercy;
And he thereat drives at her with full strength,
Pierces her in the breast
So that the sword goes through her; and she falls
Forward, upon her face,
Still always weeping; and the knight draws forth
A dagger, and opens her
By the hip-bone, and draws

Her heart out, and the rest,
And throws it to the dogs that hungrily
Devour it of a sudden. But she has lain
Not long before, as if she were not dead,
She rises up and she begins again
Her lamentable running toward the sea;
And the two dogs after her, tearing her,
Always, and always after her the knight,
Upon his horse again,
And with his sword in hand,
Always threatening her.
Tell me, can you interpret me my dream,
Smaragdi?

[*The* SLAVE, *as she listens, seems stricken with terror.*]

Are you frightened?

[GARSENDA *enters followed by the* MERCHANT *and his* BOY *carrying a pack.*]

GARSENDA

[*gaily*].

Madonna, here is the merchant with his goods.
May he come in? He is the Florentine,
Who came to Rimino yesterday with the escort
Of Messer Paolo.

[FRANCESCA, *her face suddenly flushing, shakes off her gloomy thoughts, and seems eager to seek forgetfulness of her mortal anguish ; but a kind of painful tension accompanies her volubility.*]

FRANCESCA.

Come in, come in, we are minded to renew
Our robes with the new season.

Come in, come in. I would have something made
Of sarcenet woven of many coloured threads,
Of many colours, of a hundred colours,
So that at each turn and return of light
And of sight the aspect changes ; O Smaragdi,
A raiment of pure joy!

[*The* MERCHANT *inclines humbly.*]

Good merchant, what have you to offer me?

MERCHANT.

Noble Madonna, everything that suits
With your nobility ; light taffetas,
Highly embroidered, circlet upon circlet,
Sarcenet, samite, and damask,
Grogram and bombasin,
Camlet, barracan, fustian,
Serge, Neopolitan doublets,
Sicilian tunics,
Watered silk, high or low, watered with gold
And silver thread, and waved ;
Linen of Lucca, Osta, Dondiscarte,
Of Bruges, of Tournai, and of Terremonde,
And of Mostavolieri in Normandy,
Fine serge from Como, changeable taffeta,
Cloth of silk worked in trees and squares and eyelets
And patterns toothed and fish-boned,
Velvets of every sort
And every make,
Velvets one piled, and two piled, and three piled.

[GARSENDA *bursts out laughing.*]

FRANCESCA

Enough! enough! And have you found a warehouse
In Rimino for so many goods?

MERCHANT.

I am
Giotto di Bernarduccio Boninsegni,
The agent of the Company of Piero
Di Niccolaio degli Oricellari,
That has its thousand samples in the warehouses
Of Calimala and of Calimaruzza,
And sends its agents over all the west,
As far as Ireland, and, in the Levant,
As far as the Cattaio, noble Madonna.

[GARSENDA *laughs. The* MERCHANT *turns and looks at her*]

GARSENDA.

A florin or two, eh?
You lent to Prester John,
(Poor wretch!) or to the Khan of Babylon.

[*The* MERCHANT *opens the pack before* FRANCESCA, *who stands at the reading desk, and exhibits his goods.*]

MERCHANT.

We go to Armalecco, to buy vair,
Sable and ermine,
And marten-skins, and lynx, and other skins ;
And to buy woollen too,
To the monasteries of England, and to Chinna,
To Bilignass, Croccostrande, and Isticchi,
To Diolacresca, Giúttebi, and Bufeltro,
In Cornwall.

[GARSENDA *laughs.*]

GARSENDA.

Then you saw
King Mark in Cornwall, then

The fair-haired Iseult bought brocades from you,
Sky-coloured, of a surety? Or you carried
Her Tristan, hidden in your pack of goods,
Into her chamber?

MERCHANT.

They say that in Romagna
All fowling, nay, all gulling, is permitted ;
But the blackbird has already crossed the stream
And his mate has crossed the Po already.

GARSENDA.

Shafts
Of Florence make and Lombard : bastard shafts.
They neither shine nor sting,
Because I do not know them.

[FRANCESCA *seems intent on turning over the stuffs.*]

FRANCESCA.

This is good,
Brocade with golden pomegranates. And how,
Giotto, did you come here to Rimino?

MERCHANT.

Noble Madonna, full of perils is
The life of merchants. Needs must be we take
Every occasion that is offered us.
I, by good fortune, chanced to come upon
The escort of the noble Messer Paolo,
And had good leave to follow it in safety.
So swift a journey may I never make

Again ; with Messer Paolo you ride
The whole day long, and never sleep at all.

[FRANCESCA *feels over the stuffs, outwardly calm, but an unconquerable smile burns in her eyes.* GARSENDA *has gone down on her knees to see the stuffs.*]

FRANCESCA.

You rode so swiftly?

MERCHANT.

Without rest or stay,
With tightened bridles, if I might so put it ;
And every stream they forded, could not wait
Until the flood had ebbed. And Messer Paolo
Laboured his horse with spur in such a haste
That there was always between him and us,
A mile or so of distance. I should say
He has some urgent business here. He asked
The Commune leave of absence
After two months, or little more, that he
Had entered into office ; truth it is
That the whole city sorrows at it, never
A more accustomed and more civil knight
Was Captain of the People there in Florence.

FRANCESCA.

I will take this brocade.

MERCHANT.

Good, very good,
Madonna, And Bernardino della Porta
Of Parma, they have chosen
To take his place, is worth,
Why not so much as one hair of the head
Of Messer Paolo.

FRANCESCA.

And this samite too.

MERCHANT.

Madonna, this with patterns all of gold. . .

FRANCESCA.

Yes, I like this one too. It seems to me
You Florentines keep feast on feast, and make
The year a holiday, and care for nothing
Except for games and sports and banquetings
And dances.

MERCHANT.

Yes, Madonna, 'tis a sweet
And blessed land, our Florence : 'tis the flower
Of the others, Fiorenza!

FRANCESCA.

I will take this silk too with the silver lines.
And the Captain of the People,
Was he well liked by all the companies
Of knights and ladies?

MERCHANT.

Each rivalled with each
Of all the companies
To have his presence, as the most well-spoken
And gallant man he indeed is; but he,
By what I know, would hold himself apart,
A trifle haughtily, and rare it was
To see him at their suppers. And in time
Of Carnival, in Santa Felicita
Beyond the Arno, I know by Messer Betto
De'Rossi that they made a company,
A thousand men or more, all dressed in white,
And Messer Paolo by this company

Was chosen Lord of Love,
But he would not consent . . .

FRANCESCA.

Here, this shot sarcenet
And this buff-coloured cotton. You were saying,
Giotto . . .

[GARSENDA *takes the stuffs selected, and puts them aside, first holding them up to the light.*]

MERCHANT.

I have seen him sometimes go about
With Guido of the Messers Cavalcante
Dei Cavalcanti ; he that is, they say,
One of the best logicians in the world,
And a most manifest
Natural philosopher,
And, as they say, he seeks,
Among the tombs, to find
There never was a God.

FRANCESCA.

Garsenda, you may have this violet samite.

GARSENDA.

O Madonna, much thanks!

MERCHANT.

'Tis a fine violet,
One of the finest colours of the dye.

FRANCESCA.

And for you, Smaragdi? You were saying, Giotto . . .

MERCHANT.

Often he had with him
Good singers and good players, specially

Casella da Pistoia the musician,
A master in the art of singing songs
Of love . . .

FRANCESCA.

For you, Smaragdi, you shall have
This green-brown serge. And Altichiara too
And Biancofiore, each of you must have
A new dress.

MERCHANT.

This, Madonna, is a colour
Of the newest fashion, it is called the seamew,
A very marvel, with its golden bunches;
Mona Giuglia degli Adimari, the other week,
Bought from me full ten yards of it. And this
With the goose pattern. Capon's foot, bear's ear,
Young pigeon, angel's wing,
Iris, corn-flower, new colours . . .

[FRANCESCA *rises impetuously, as if breaking some constraint.*]

FRANCESCA.

Merchant, leave it,
And I will choose at leisure.

[*She turns towards the window and looks out on the shining sea, shading her eyes with her hand.*]

How the sun
Is strong, this March, and fierce!
There goes a little ship with a red sail!
Here are the swallows coming back in flocks!

GARSENDA

[*to the* MERCHANT].

How long shall you be staying in Rimino?

MERCHANT.

Three days. And then I have to make my way
To Barletta and from Barletta I take ship
For Cyprus.

[*The* SLAVE *lights up, hearing the name of her country.*]

GARSENDA.

Listen, listen,
Smaragdi!

SLAVE
[*anxiously*].

Do you go to Cyprus, merchant?

MERCHANT.

I go there yearly. We have warehouses
At Famagosta, and there yearly sell
Thousands and thousands besants' worth of goods.
Are you from Cyprus?

SLAVE.

Salute for me the Mount Chionodes,
His head in snow and olives at his feet;
And drink for me at the spring of Chitria
A draught for my heart's sake.

FRANCESCA
[*turning*].

"And Cyprus I would make for,
And at Limisso anchor,
And land my sailors for a kiss, my captains
For love!"

[*Instruments and merry voices are heard preluding while she goes towards the bed, droopingly, as if to lie down on it.*]

SLAVE.

And who is king there? Sire Ughetto?

MERCHANT.

Ughetto died young, Ugo di Lusignano,
His cousin, is king now. And there have been
Most evil deeds,
And poisonings of women,
And treachery of barons and the plague,
Locusts and earthquakes,
And Venus, queen of devils, has appeared.

[*The sounds of music and voices and laughter come nearer.* FRANCESCA *lies back on the bed between the half-closed curtains.*]

[*The* WOMEN, *with the exception of* ADONELLA, *enter, followed by the* DOCTOR, *the* ASTROLOGER, *the* JESTER *and the* MUSICIANS, *who tune their instruments and prelude on them. The* DOCTOR *wears a dressing-gown, down to the heels, of a dark tan-colour; the* ASTROLOGER *a green-brown robe and a black turban striped with yellow; the* JESTER *a scarlet jerkin. The* MUSICIANS *go up on their gallery, and range themselves in order.*

ALTICHIARA.

Madonna, here is Maestro Almodoro.

ALDA.

And we have found the astrologer, Madonna.

BIANCOFIORE.

And the Jester too, Gian Figo, that procures
Recipes against melancholy with songs
And stories and the dust of No-Man's Land.

ALDA.

And the voices and the players
On bagpipe, flute and lute,
Rebec and monochord.

[*Standing upright between the curtains*, FRANCESCA *looks before her as if bewildered, neither smiling nor speaking.*]

BIANCOFIORE
[*coming forward*].

Here is the garland
Of violets. May it chase your melancholy!

[*She offers it to her gracefully.* FRANCESCA *takes it, while* ALTICHIARA *takes the mirror from the table and holds it up before her face as she puts on the garland. The* SLAVE *slowly goes out.*]

GARSENDA.

O Maestro Almodoro,
Galen, Hippocrates, and Avicenna
Returned to earth inside one doctor's gown,
Can you tell us what is melancholy?

[*The* DOCTOR *places himself in their midst, and assumes a solemn air.*]

DOCTOR.

Melancholy
Is a dark humour many call black bile,
And it is cold and dry,
And has its situation in the spine;
Its nature is of the earth
And of the autumn. Nec dubium est quidem
Melancholicus morbus
Ab impostore Diabolo. . .

[*The* JESTER *puts himself in front of him, covering him. The* WOMEN *and the* MUSICIANS *laugh and whisper.*]

JESTER.

When
Your devil was born, my devil had found his legs.
Melancholy is to drink as the Germans do,
Madonna; to backbite as the Greeks do,
To sing as the French do,
To dance as the Moors do,
To sleep as the English do,
And to stand steady like
Messere Ferragunze the Cordelier.
Madonna, I have had from you those two
Pieces of scarlet in advance: but see,
The jerkin that was new has become old.
Have you two other pieces, may it please you,
Of velvet?

[*The* WOMEN *laugh. He eyes the merchant's wares, scattered over the couch.*]

GARSENDA.

The Astrologer! Speak now,
Astrologer of Syria who sees all things!

[*The bearded* ASTROLOGER *puts on a gloomy look and speaks with a voice that seems to come from a deep cave.*]

ASTROLOGER.

All darts he sees not, who sees every dart;
But he who blindly aims against the heart
Takes aim from thence, whence doth all life depart.

JESTER.

And I believe not in your art.

[FRANCESCA *looks sharply at the* SARACEN, *as if fearing something.*]

FRANCESCA.

What do you mean by this dark riddle? Speak,
Maestro Isacco, explain.

ASTROLOGER.

Lady, who inward looks,
Looks not, but he who wills that which he looks.

JESTER.

And yet the man of Friuli has said:
He who wants woman wants a lord and master,
And he who wants a lord and master wants—
Catch who catch can! And then
In the book of Madam Mogias of Egypt,
That is called the Book of Piercing to the Heart,
It is declared that woman's enemies
Are seventeen—

[ADONELLA *enters, carrying five garlands of white narcissi, hanging from a gold wire that binds them together.*]

ADONELLA.

Madonna, the falconer
Has called the falcon back. Some of his feathers
Are bent or broken a little ; but warm water
And a soft bandage will soon set them right.

ASTROLOGER.

The falcon's beak thou shalt not shear or break,
But scanty clippings take;

For these, well mixed with wool, long talons
make.

FRANCESCA.

You speak in riddles, then,
To-day, Maestro Isacco ?

ASTROLOGER.

Not every one who speaketh speaks, but he
Who sleeps must silent be ;
Evils in life and truth in prophecy.

JESTER.

So may it be, amen! Bring in the bier.
O Saracen Isacco,
You are a very great astronomer ;
You prophesy, besides ;
But you must make a little matter plain.
Tell me, which is the easier to know,
The things that are now past,
Or else the things that are to come ?

ASTROLOGER.

O fool,
Who does not know the things that he has seen,
The things that are behind ?

JESTER.

Good, very good ; we'll see how well you know
them.
Now tell me this,
What were you doing on the last March calends,
A year ago !

[*The* ASTROLOGER *thinks.*]

Well, then, six months ago ?

[*The* ASTROLOGER *thinks. The* WOMEN *laugh. The* JESTER *speaks rapidly.*]

I will ask you, then, one last time: can you tell me
What weather it was three months ago?

[*The* ASTROLOGER *thinks and stares before him. The* JESTER *plucks him by the robe.*]

Isacco,
Don't cast nativities, you need not gape,
Stand steady. Now, what ship
Came here, a month ago? What ship set sail?
What do you gape at? Did you eat indoors
Or out of doors a fortnight since?

ASTROLOGER.

Wait, wait
A little.

JESTER.

Wait! What? But I will not wait.
Come now, what were you doing,
A week ago to-day?

ASTROLOGER.

Give me a little respite.

JESTER.

Why, what respite
Should such as I give such as you who know
The things that are to come? What did you eat
Four days ago?

ASTROLOGER.

Ah, I will tell you that.

JESTER.

What did you say?

ASTROLOGER.

You are in such haste.

ELEONORA DUSE
AS FRANCESCA DA RIMINI

JESTER.

What haste? Well, tell me now, what did you eat
Yesterday morning? Tell me!

[*The* ASTROLOGER, *annoyed, turns his back upon him. He plucks him by the sleeve.*]

Stop! Look at me a moment!
I lay you ten to one you do not know
If you are wide awake or if you dream.

ASTROLOGER.

I know I do not sleep, and that you are
The greatest fool now living in the world!

JESTER.

But I assure you that you do not know.
Come here. Don't go like that against the wind
Of Mongibello. Tell me, have you not
Hundreds of times gone up and down the stairs
Of the belfry-tower of Santa Colomba? Well,
How many stairs are there? Come here, I say!
Don't run away from me. Have you ever eaten
Medlars? How many pips are in a medlar?

[*The infuriated* ASTROLOGER *frees himself from the grip of the* JESTER, *amidst much laughter.*]

Then if you don't know that,
How can you know things that are in the sky,
And in the hearts of women, and in hair?
Find a cordwainer, bid him make a rope
Out of your beard, and hang you to a star.

BIANCOFIORE.

Madonna has smiled!
Gian Figo has made even Madonna smile!

Go, go, dear doctor, to your house again,
And take your medicine and your Latin with you,
To-day is the March calends! Song means dance
To-day, and dance means song.
Play, Simonetto, play!

[*The* MUSICIANS *begin a prelude. Those standing near go to the back, so as to leave room for the dance.* ADONELLA *unlooses the gold wire, and distributes the garlands of narcissi to her companions, who put them on; and retains for herself the one that bears two swallows' wings.* ALDA *takes out of a little bag four painted wooden swallows that have a kind of small handle under the breast, and gives one to each of her companions; who, standing ready for the dance, hold them each raised in the left hand.* ADONELLA *whistles, in imitation of the chirruping of swallows, and, while the other four dance and sing, she utters at intervals, according to the rhythm, the loud chirping that heralds the spring.*]

ALDA.

Fresh, fresh, in the calends of March,
O swallows, coming home
Fresh from the quiet lands beyond the sea;
First to bring back the great good messages
Of joy, and first to taste the good wild scent.
O creature of pure joy,
Come in your garments white and black, fly hither,
And bring your springtide gladness to our dance!

ALTICHIARA.

March comes, and February
Goes with the wind to-day;
Bring out your taffety
And put the vair away.
And come with me, I pray,
Across the streams in flood,
Under the branching wood that leans along,
With dancing and with song in company
With fleet-foot lovers, or upon the lea
Gather the violets,
Where the grass smells more sweet because her
feet,
Have passed that way, the naked feet of
Spring!

GARSENDA.

To-day the earth appears
New-wedded like a girl;
The face that the sea wears
To-day is like a pearl.
Hark, hark, is that the merle
Deep in the thicket? Hark,
How swift upsoars the lark into the sky!
The cruel wind goes by, and in his mouth
Bears ravished nests! O swallow of the south,
Thy tail's an arrow feather,
And like the twanging of a bow thy cry
Whereby the spring will strike, the hands of
Spring!

BIANCOFIORE.

O creature of delight,
Lead thou the dancing feet,
In robe of black and white,

As is thy usage sweet.
Make here thy stay, O fleet
Swallow, here in this room
Wherein is seen, in gloom or light of day,
The tale of Iseult, the fair flower of Ireland,
As here thou seest, and this shall be thy garland,
Thy nest, no prison-mesh,
Seeing that the fresh fair lady seated here
Is not Francesca, but is very—

[*The* DANCERS *return rapidly, towards* FRANCESCA *and form in a line, stretching out towards her the hand that holds the swallow, and the other; and they all sing with* BIANCOFIORE, *without interval, the last word of the stanza.*]

ALL

Spring!

[*At the beginning of the last movement the* SLAVE *appears on the threshold. As the* MUSICIANS *play the last notes, she goes up to* FRANCESCA *hurriedly and whispers to her something that suddenly disturbs her.*]

FRANCESCA
(*Impetuously*).

Biancofiore, Altichiara, Alda, Adonella,
Garsenda, for the new
Delight of this new dance,
I must give you something new:
These dresses, take them, each!

[*She picks up some of the scattered goods and gives them.*]

Here's for you, and for you!

[*The* JESTER *comes forward in a sidelong way.*]

And for you too,

Gian Figo, but no jesting.

[*The* JESTER *takes it and decamps.*]

Garsenda, take this too for the Musicians,
They can make jackets of it,
With stripes of red and yellow. And see, too, Merchant
You set aside two lengths of some good serge
For Maestro Almodoro, and Maestro Isacco.
Now go, I have given you something, all of you,
For the March calends' sake. Go now, and, going,
Sing in the court the song of the March swallows.
You must come back again, Merchant; Garsenda
Will bring you word. You may leave your wares here now.
Go, and be merry, until vesper-time;
Adonella, lead the way into the court.
A happy spring to you!

[*The* MUSICIANS *come down from their gallery, playing, and go out. The* JESTER *skips after them.* ALL *the others bow before* FRANCESCA *and take the gifts they have received, following the* MUSICIANS *with whispering and laughter. The* SLAVE *remains, busy wrapping up the wares in bundles.* FRANCESCA *abandons herself to her anxiety. She takes several steps, blindly; with a sudden movement, she draws the curtains of the alcove, which are half open, showing the bed. Then she sits down be-*

fore the reading-desk, and glances at the open book, but, in turning, the train of her dress catches in the lute, which falls, and lies on the ground. She trembles.]

No, no, Smaragdi! Run, and tell him not
To come!

[*The sounds die away in the distance. The* SLAVE, *having finished, goes towards the door.* FRANCESCA *takes a step towards her as if to call her back.*]

Smaragdi!

[*The* SLAVE *goes out.*]

[*After a few moments, a hand raises the curtain, and* PAOLO MALATESTA *appears. The door closes behind him*]. *As* PAOLO *and* FRANCESCA *gaze at one another, for a moment, without finding words, both change colour. The sound of* MUSIC *dies away through the palace. The room is gilded by the rays of the setting sun, which shine through the long window.*]

FRANCESCA.

Welcome, my lord and kinsman.

PAOLO

I have come,
Hearing a sound of music, to bring greetings,
My greetings of return.

FRANCESCA.

You have come back
Speedily, sir; indeed with the first swallow.
My women even now
Were singing a new song that they have made

To welcome March. And there was also here
The merchant out of Florence, who had come
Among your following. Of him I had
Tidings of you.

PAOLO.

But I, of you, no tidings,
None, I heard nothing there,
Nothing of you at all,
From that day onward, when, one perilous night
You put a cup of wine into my hands,
And said to me, "farewell!"
And said to me, "God-speed!"

FRANCESCA.

I have no memory,
My lord, concerning this. I have prayed much.

PAOLO.

You have forgotten then?

FRANCESCA.

I have prayed much.

PAOLO.

And I have suffered much.
If it be true that he who suffers conquers,
I think I must needs conquer. . . .

FRANCESCA.

What?

PAOLO.

My fate,
Francesca.

FRANCESCA.

And yet you have come back?

PAOLO.

I have come back
To live.

FRANCESCA.

Not to die now?

PAOLO.

Ah, you remember
The death I was to die,
And you that would not! So much, at the least,
You have remembered.

[*She draws back towards the window, as if withdrawing herself from his scarcely repressed violence.*]

FRANCESCA.

Paolo, give me peace!
It is so sweet a thing to live forgetting,
But one hour only, and be no more tossed,
Out of the tempest.
Do not call back, I pray,
The shadow of that time in this fresh light
That slakes my thirst at last
Like that long draught
That at the ford I drank,
Out of the living water.
And now, I desire now
To think my soul has left
That shore to come into this sheltering shore,
Where music and where hope are sisters; so
To forget all the sorrow that has been
Yesterday, and shall be
To-morrow, and so let
All of my life, and all the veins of it,
And all the days of it,

And all old things in it, far-away things,
But for one hour, one hour,
Slip away quietly, a quiet tide,
Unto that sea,
Even these eyes might behold smilingly,
Were it not hidden by the tears that tremble
And do not fall. O peace, peace in that sea
That was so wild with waves
Yesterday, and to-day is like a pearl.
Give me peace!

PAOLO.

It is the voice of spring
I hear, and from your lips the music runs
Over the world, that I have seemed to hear,
Riding against the wind,
Sing in the voice of the wind,
At every turn of the way,
At every glade, and high
On the hill-tops, and on the edges of the woods,
And under them the streams,
When my desire bent back,
Burning with breath, the mane of my wild horse,
Over the saddle-bow, and the soul lived,
In the swiftness of that flight,
On swiftness,
Like a torch carried in the wind, and all
The thoughts of all my soul, save one, save one,
Were all blown backward, spent
Like sparks behind me.

FRANCESCA.

Ah, Paolo, like sparks
All your words are, and still they take no rest,
And all your soul lives still

In the strong wind and swiftness of your coming,
And drags me with it, and I am full of fear.
I pray you, I pray you now,
That you will give me peace
For this hour only,
My fair friend, my sweet friend,
That I may quiet and put to sleep in me
The old sick pain, and forget all the rest;
Only bring back into my eyes the first.
Look that took hold on me out of your face,
Unknown to me ; for these dry eyelids have
No need of any healing but that dew,
Only to bring back and to have in them
Again the miracle of that first look ;
And they will feel that grace has come to them,
As they felt once, out of the heart of a dream,
The coming near of the dawn ;
And feel that they are to be comforted,
Perhaps in the shade
Of the new garland.

PAOLO.

And so garlanded
With violets I saw you yesterday
In a meadow, as I stayed,
Pausing in journeying,
And being alone, and having far outstripped
My escort. I could hear
Only the champing bit
Of my horse pasturing, and see from there
The towers of Meldola in a wood. And all
Palpitated with you
In the high morning. And you came to me
With violets, and returning to your lips

I heard again a word that you had spoken,
Saying : I pardon you, and with much love!

FRANCESCA.

That word was spoken
And perfect joy awaits upon the word.

[PAOLO'S *eyes wander over the room.*]

Ah, do not look around
Upon these things,
Silent, as if with joy,
And only full of sorrow and of shame.
No autumn withered them,
They shall not be awakened with the spring.
Look on the sea, the sea
That has borne witness for us once with God
To certain words once spoken, vast and calm
And shining where the battle came between,
And silent where the rage of clamour came
Between, and one sail passed upon the sea,
Going alone upon its way, like this,
See, yonder? And our souls
Were tried, as if with fire.
But now sit here, upon the window-seat,
And not with weapons now for killing men,
But without cruelty. See, Paolo,
With this mere sprig of basil.

[*She takes a cluster from her head, and offers it to him; as he steps nearer, his foot strikes against the catch of the trap-door, and he stops.*]

You have struck your foot
Against the ring of the trap-door. It leads
From here into another room beneath.

[PAOLO *stoops to look at it.*]

PAOLO.

Ah, you can go from here into a room
Beneath.

FRANCESCA

[*Giving him the sprig of basil*].

Come, take it, smell it; it is good.
Smaragdi planted it in memory
Of Cyprus, in this vase;
And when she waters it,
She sings: "Under your feet
I spread sweet basil,
I bid you sleep there,
I bid you pluck it,
I bid you smell it,
And remember the giver!"
At Florence all the women
Have their sweet basil on the window-sill.
Do you not know? But come,
Will you not tell me something of your life?
Sit here, and tell me something of yourself,
How you have lived.

PAOLO.

Why do you ask of me
To live the misery of my life twice over?
All that was joy to others was to me
Sorrow and heaviness. One only thing,
Music, could ever give me pleasant hours.
I went sometimes to a great singer's house,
He was by name Casella,
And there were met many of gentle birth,
Among them Guido Cavalcanti, and these
Were wont to make rhymes in the vulgar tongue;
And there was Ser Brunetto,

Returned from Paris, wise
With rhetoric of the schools,
Also a youth
Of the Alighieri, Dante was his name,
And I much loved this youth, he was so full
Of thoughts of love and sorrow,
So burning and so loverlike for song.
And something like a healing influence passed
Out of his heart to mine,
That seemed shut up in me; for the exceeding
And too much sweetness hid
Sometimes within the song moved him to weep
Silently, silent tears,
And seeing his weeping, I too wept with him.

[*Her eyes fill with tears and her voice trembles.*]

FRANCESCA.

You wept?

PAOLO.

Francesca!

FRANCESCA.

Wept? Ah, Paolo mine,
Blessed be he that taught your heart such tears,
Such tears! I will pray always for his peace.
For now I see you, now I see you again
As you were then, sweet friend.
The grace has come with healing to my eyes.

[*She appears as if transfigured with perfect joy. With a slow movement she takes the garland from her head and lays it on the open book beside her*].

PAOLO.

Why do you take the garland from your head?

FRANCESCA.

Because it was not you who gave it me.
I gave you once a rose
From that sarcophagus.
But now, poor flowers, I feel
Your freshness is all spent!

[PAOLO *rises, and goes up to the reading desk and touches the violets.*]

PAOLO.

'Tis true! Do you remember? on that night
Of fire and blood, you asked of me the gift
Of a fair helmet; and I gave it you:
'Twas finely tempered.
The steel and gold of it have never known
What rust is, soiling. And you let it fall.
Do you remember?
I picked it up, and I have held it dear
As a king's crown.
Since then, when I have set it on my head,
I feel twice bold, and there is not a thought
Within my heart that is not as a flame.

[*He bends over the book.*]

Ah, listen, the first words that meet my eye!
"Made richer by that gift than had you given him
The gift of all the world."
What book is this?

FRANCESCA.

The famous history
Of Lancelot of the Lake.

[*She rises and goes over to the reading-desk.*]

PAOLO.

And have you read
The book all through?

FRANCESCA.

I have but
Come in my reading to this point.

PAOLO.

To where?
Here, where the mark is?
[*He reads.*]
". . . . . but you ask of me
Nothing . . . . ." Will you go on?

FRANCESCA.

Look how the sea is growing white with light!

PAOLO.

Will you not read the page with me, Francesca?

FRANCESCA.

Look yonder, how a flight
Of swallows comes, and coming sets a shadow
On the white sea!

PAOLO.

Will you not read, Francesca?

FRANCESCA.

And there is one sail, and so red it seems
Like fire.

PAOLO

[*Reading*].
" 'Assuredly, my lady' says
Thereat Galeotto, 'he is not so hot,
He does not ask you any single thing
For love of you, because he fears, but I
Make suit to you for him; and know that I

Had never asked it of you, but that you
Were better off for it, seeing it is
The richest treasure you shall ever compass.'
Whereat says she . . . ."

[PAOLO *draws* FRANCESCA *gently by the hand.*]

But now, will you not read
What she says ? Will you not be Guenevere?
See now how sweet they are,
Your violets
That you have cast away! Come, read a little.

[*Their heads lean together over the book.*]

FRANCESCA

[*Reading*].

"Whereat says she: 'This know I well, and I
Will do whatever thing you ask of me.'
And Galeotto answers her: 'Much thanks,
Lady! I ask you that you give to him
Your love . . . . .'"

[*She stops.*]

PAOLO.

But read on.

FRANCESCA.

No, I cannot see
The words.

PAOLO.

Read on. It says: "Assuredly . . . . ."

FRANCESCA.

"'Assuredly,' says she, 'I promise it,
But let him be mine own and I all his,
And let there be set straight all crooked things
And evil . . . .'" Enough, Paolo.

PAOLO

[*Reading: hoarsely and tremulously.*]

"'Lady!' says he, 'much thanks, but kiss him
then,
Now, and before my face, for a beginning
Of a true love . . . . .'" You, you! what does
she say?
Now, what does she say? Here.

[*Their white faces lean over the book, until their cheeks almost touch.*]

FRANCESCA

[*Reading*].

"Says she : 'For what
Shall I be then entreated. But I will it
More than he wills it . . .'"

PAOLO

[*Following brokenly*].

"And they draw apart
And the queen looks on him and sees that he
Cannot take heart on him to do aught more.
Thereat she takes him by the chin, and slowly
Kisses him on the mouth . . . . ."

[HE *makes the same movement towards* FRANCESCA, *and kisses her. As their mouths separate,* FRANCESCA *staggers and falls back on the cushions.*]

FRANCESCA

[*Faintly*].

No, Paolo!

ACT IV.

An octagonal hall, of gray stone, with five of its sides in perspective. High up, on the bare stone, is a frieze of unicorns on a gold background. On the wall at the back is a large window with glass panes, looking out on the mountain, furnished with benches in the recess. On the wall at right angles to it, on the right, is a grated door leading to the subterranean prison. Against the opposite wall, to the left, is a long wooden seat with a high back, in front of which is a long narrow table laid with fruit and wine. In each of the other two sides facing, is a door; the left, near the table, leads to the room of FRANCESCA, *the right to the corridor and stairs. All round are placed torchbearers of iron; on brackets are hung shoulder-belts, waist-belts, quivers, and different portions of armour; pikes, lances, halberds, spears, axes, balistas lean against them.*

[FRANCESCA *is seated at the window, and* MALATESTINO *stands at her feet.*]

FRANCESCA.

You would be justicer, Malatestino!
Your cradle, of a surety, was hewn out

From some old tree-trunk by a savage axe
That had cut many heads off before then.

MALATESTINO
[*laughs convulsively*].

Kinswoman, do I fright you?
And should I please you better
If I had had my cradle in the rose
Of a calm lute?

FRANCESCA.

You are a cruel boy to take revenge
Upon a falcon!
Why did you kill him, if you held him dear?

MALATESTINO.

Merely for justice' sake.
See, I had let him loose upon a crane,
The crane went up, the falcon followed him
And went up far above him, and under him
Saw a young eagle flying, and he took him
And struck him to the ground, and held him so
Till he had killed him.
I ran to take him, thinking him the crane,
But found it was an eagle.
Then I was angry, and struck off the head
Of the fair falcon who had killed his lord.

FRANCESCA.

It was a foolish deed.

MALATESTINO.

But he had killed
His lord. I did but justice.

FRANCESCA.

It was a wicked folly, Malatestino.

MALATESTINO.

The fool shall pass, and with the fool his folly,
And the time passes, but not every time.

FRANCESCA.

Why do you speak so strangely?
You are athirst for blood
Always, always at watch,
The enemy of all things. In all your words
There is a secret menace ;
Like a wild beast you bite
And tear and claw whatever comes your way.
Where were you born? Your mother gave you milk
As to another? And you are so young!
The down is scarcely shadowed on your cheek.

MALATESTINO
[*With sudden violence*].

You are a goad to me,
The thought of you is like a goad to me,
Always. You are my wrath.

[FRANCESCA *rises and moves away from the window, as if to escape from a snare. She stands near the wall against which arms are heaped up.*]

FRANCESCA.

Malatestino, enough! Have you no shame?
Your brother will be here.

MALATESTINO
[*following her*].

You strain me like a bow,
That vibrates in an hour
A thousand times, and pierces at a venture.

Your hand is terrible,
That holds my force in it,
And casts it out to wound where it has flown.
I fly you, and you follow.
You are with me suddenly,
Like a sharp storm of rain,
In the fields and on the ways,
When I go out
Against the enemy.
I breathe you when I breathe the dust of battles.
The cloud that rises from the trampled earth
Takes on your very form,
And you live and breathe and you dissolve again
Under the pawing of the panting horses
In the tracks that redden and fill up with blood.
I will clasp you, I will clasp you now at last!

[FRANCESCA *retreats along the wall until she comes to the grated door.*]

FRANCESCA.

You do not touch me, madman, or I call
Your brother! Get you gone. I pity you.
You are a boy. If you would not be whipped,
Get you gone. You are a boy,
A wicked boy.

MALATESTINO.

Whom would you call?

FRANCESCA.

Your brother.

MALATESTINO.

Which?

[FRANCESCA *starts, hearing a cry rise up from below, through the door against which she is standing.*]

FRANCESCA.

Who cried there? Did you not hear it?

MALATESTINO.

One
Who has to die.

FRANCESCA.

Montagna
Dei Parcitadi?

[*Another cry comes from the prison.*]

MALATESTINO.

I too will say: Enough!
Enough, Francesca, to-day you seal your fate.

FRANCESCA.

Ah, now I cannot hear him; but at night
He howls, howls like a wolf;
His crying rises to me in my room.
What have you done to him?
Have you put him to the torture?

MALATESTINO.

Listen to me. Giovanni
Sets out at Vespers for the Podesteria
Of Pesaro. You have prepared for him
Food for the journey.

[*He points to the table.*]

Listen. I can give him
Food for another journey.

FRANCESCA.

What do you mean?

MALATESTINO.

Look well at me. I can still see with one.

FRANCESCA.

What do you mean? You threaten me? You net
Some treachery against your brother.

MALATESTINO.

Treachery?
I would have thought, kinswoman, that such a word
Had burnt your tongue; I see
Your lips are scathless, though
A little paler. I but spoke at random.
My judgment was at fault. Only I say
This one time more . . . .

[*The crying of the* PRISONER *is again heard.*]

FRANCESCA

[*Trembling with horror*].

How he cries! How he cries!
Who tortures him, or what new agony
Have you found out for him?
Have you walled him up alive? Will he cry so
All his life long? Go, put an end to it,
And take him from his torture.
I will not hear his crying any more.

MALATESTINO.

Well, I will go. I will see that you shall have
A quiet night and an untroubled sleep,
Because to-morrow you must sleep alone,
While my good brother rides to Pesaro.

[*He goes up to the wall and chooses an axe from among the weapons piled up against it.*]

FRANCESCA.

What are you doing?

MALATESTINO.

I?
I would be justicer,
And by your wish and will,
Kinswoman.

[*He examines the blade of the weapon; then unbolts the barred door, which opens upon black darkness.*]

FRANCESCA.

You are going to kill him? Ah,
Wild beast, but you have lived too long, I think,
Since I bound up your wound for you, and you
Raved at your father. Still I hear you. Then
You bit the hand that gave you medicine,
Cared for you in your sickness, soothed your pain.
Accursed be the hour in which I bent
Over your pillow to give ease to you!

MALATESTINO.

Francesca, listen, Francesca: even so sure
As death is in the point of this good weapon
I hold here in my hand, so sure is life
In that one word
You still may say to me,
Full-blooded life, do you not understand?
And full of winds, and full of conquering days.

[FRANCESCA *replies slowly, in an equable voice, as in a momentary respite from horror and anxiety.*]

FRANCESCA.

What is the word? Who is there that could say it?
You live in a loud noise,

But where I live is silence. The prisoner
Is not so far and lonely
As you are far and lonely, O poor blind
Slaughterman, drunk with shoutings, and with
blows!
But fate is very silent.

MALATESTINO.

Ah, if you could but see the countenance
Of the overhanging fate!
There is a wretched knot within my head,
A knot of thoughts like pent-up lightnings: soon
They will break out. But listen,
Listen! If your hand will but touch my hand,
If your hair will lean over me again,
Over my fever, and . . .
[*A more prolonged cry is heard from below.*]

FRANCESCA.

O horror! horror!
[*She moves back to the embrasure of the window, sits down, and puts her elbows on her knees, and her head between her hands.*]

MALATESTINO

[*Looking aside at her*].

This shall be from you.

[*He takes down a torch, puts the axe on the ground, takes the steel, strikes it, and lights the torch, while he speaks.*]

I go. You will not hear him any more.
I will see that you shall have
A quiet night and an untroubled sleep,
And I will give my father quiet too;

He fears his flight. And I would have Giovanni
In passing by Gradara, give him this
Most certain token.
O kinswoman, good vespers!

FRANCESCA *remains motionless as if hearing nothing.*

He picks up the weapon and goes into the darkness with his silent cat-like step, holding the lighted torch in his left hand. The little door remains open. FRANCESCA *rises and watches the light fade away in the opening; suddenly she runs to the door, and stops, shuddering. The barred door grates in the silence. She turns, and moves away with slow steps, her head bent, as if under a heavy weight.*]

FRANCESCA

[*In a low voice, to herself*].

And an untroubled sleep!

[*Through the great door on the right is heard the harsh voice of* GIANCIOTTO. FRANCESCA *stops suddenly.*]

GIOVANNI.

Look you for Messer Paolo my brother,
And tell him I set out for Pesaro
In an hour's time from now,
And that I wait him.

[*He enters fully armed. Seeing his wife, he goes up to her.*]

Ah my dear lady, you are waiting me!
Why do you tremble, why are you so pale?

[*He takes her hands.*]

And you are cold too, cold as if with fear.
But why?

FRANCESCA.

Malatestino
Had scarcely entered when I heard again
The crying of the prisoner,
Who cries these many days so horribly
Out of the earth; and, seeing me distraught,
Flamed into anger and went suddenly
Down to the prison by the door there, armed
With a great axe, saying that he would kill him,
Against the express commandments of his father
That fretted him too much.
Cruel he is, your brother, my good lord,
And does not love me.

GIANCIOTTO.

Do not tremble, lady.
Where has your valiance gone? But now you were
Fearless among the fighters,
And saw men fall with arrows in their throats,
And flung about the Greek fire in your hands.
Why does the life then of an enemy
So greatly trouble you? and a cry affright you,
Or an axe brandished?

FRANCESCA.

To fight in battle is a lovely thing,
But secret slaying in the dark I hate.

GIANCIOTTO.

Malatestino tired of keeping watch
So long, and so long waiting for the ransom
That the old Parcitade would not pay,

The old foul miser that in taking flight
Took with him certain rights and privileges
Of the Commune at Rimino . . . But why
Do you say he does not love you?

FRANCESCA.

I do not know. It seems so.

GIANCIOTTO.

Is he unkind with you?

FRANCESCA.

He is a boy, and like
Young mastiffs, he must bite. But come, my lord,
Take food and drink
Before you go your journey.

GIANCIOTTO.

But perhaps
Malatestino . . .

FRANCESCA.

Come, why do you think
Of what I said but lightly? "Heart of metal,
Tough liver:" I remember your own word,
And when you said it. He will love his horse
Until the horse falls sick;
His armour, till the steel begins to wear.
I have no mind to trouble you with him,
My lord. 'Tis almost vespers.
Come, here is food and drink. Do you mean to go
The way of the seashore?

[GIANCIOTTO *is moody, while he follows* FRANCESCA *towards the spread table. He takes off his basnet, unclasps his gorget, and gives them to his wife, who sets them down on a seat, with sudden graceful movements, talking rapidly*].

You will have all the freshness of the night.
It is September, and the nights are soft;
Just before midnight the moon rises. When
Do you reach Pesaro,
Messere il Podestà?

GIANCIOTTO.

To-morrow at the third hour,
For I must stay a little with my father
In passing through Gradara.

[*He unbuckles his sword-belt and gives it to his wife.*]

FRANCESCA.

Is it for long that you must stay at Pesaro,
Before you come again?

[*The terrible cry of* MONTAGNA *is heard from below.* FRANCESCA *shudders, and lets fall the sword, which slips from its scabbard.*]

GIANCIOTTO.

It is done now.
Do not be frightened, lady. There will be
Nothing but silence now. May God so take
The heads of all our enemies! From this forth
There shall no wind root into Rimino
This evil seed between the stones of it.
And may God scatter it out of all Romagna
In this most bloody year, if it so be
He wills to have his holy Easter held
By the Guelfs of Calboli with the Ghibelline blood

Of Aldobrandin degli Argogliosi!
[*He stoops and picks up the bare blade.*]
Pope
Martino is dead and good King Carlo went
Before him into paradise. That's ill!
As for this Pietro di Stefano that Onorio
Sends us for governor,
I doubt him, he's no friend,
He's not a Polentani, not your father's,
Francesca. We shall still have need to keep
Our swords unsheathed, and eyes in all our swords.

[*He puts himself on guard, then looks along the blade from the hilt.*]

This is inflexible!
[*He puts it back in its scabbard.*]

FRANCESCA.

Give it to me, my lord,
I will not let it fall
Twice over. And sit down, take food and drink.

[*He gives her the sword and sits down on the bench before the table.*]

GIANCIOTTO.

Good so, my own dear lady.
I talk of war to you, and now I think
That I have never given you a flower.
Ah, we are hard. I give you arms in heaps
To hold in those white hands,
Malatestino gave to you at least
A falcon. Paolo gives you
Flowers perhaps. The Captain of the People
Learnt all the courteous virtues in his Florence,

But left his force upon the banks of Arno
And now is more in love with idleness
Than any labour. He is always with
His music-makers.

[*He breaks the bread and pours out the wine, while* FRANCESCA *sits besides him, at the table, with her hands on the hilt of the sword.*]

But you,
Francesca, love your chamber-music too.
Are not your women ever tired of singing?
Their voices must have covered
The cries of Parcitade,
Surely? You turn the tower
Of the Malatesti
Into a singing wood of nightingales.

[*He eats and drinks.*]

FRANCESCA.

I and Samaritana,
My sister, at Ravenna, in our home,
Lived always, always in the midst of singing.
Our mother had indeed a throat of gold.
From our first infancy
Music flowed over us and bent our souls
As the water bends the grass upon the bank.
And our mother said to me :
Sweet singing can put out all harmful things.

GIANCIOTTO.

My mother said to us.
Do you know what woman is a proper woman?
She that in spinning thinks upon the spindle,
She that in spinning spins without a knot,
She that in spinning lets not fall the spindle,

She that winds thread in order about thread,
She that knows when the spindle is full or half-way.

FRANCESCA.

Then why did you not seek for such a woman,
My lord, through all the country?

[*A knocking is heard at the little barred door.* FRANCESCA *rises to her feet, drops the sword on the table and turns to go out.*]

Malatestino back!
I will not wait to see him.

THE VOICE OF MALATESTINO.

Who has shut it?
Kinswoman are you there? Have you shut me in?

[*He kicks at the door.*]

GIANCIOTTO.

Wait, wait, and I will open!

THE VOICE OF MALATESTINO.

Ah, Giovanni!
Open, and I will bring you
A good ripe heavy fruit,
Food for your journey:
A ripe September fig.
And how it weighs!

[GIANCIOTTO *goes to the door to open it.* FRANCESCA *follows his limping steps for some instants with her eyes, then moves towards the door that leads to her rooms, and goes out.*]

Be quick!

GIANCIOTTO.

Why, here I am.

[*He opens the door, and* MALATESTINO *appears in the narrow doorway holding in his left hand the lighted torch, in his right, by a knotted cord, the head of* MONTAGNA *wrapped in a cloth.*]

MALATESTINO

[*Handing the torch to his brother*].

Here, brother, put it out.

[GIOVANNI *stamps out the flame under his foot.*]

Was not your wife

With you?

GIANCIOTTO

[*Roughly*].

She was with me?

What do you want of her?

MALATESTINO.

Ah, then you know

What fruit it is I am bringing to your table?

GIANCIOTTO.

Did you not fear to disobey our father?

MALATESTINO.

Feel how it weighs! now feel!

[*He hands the bundle to* GIOVANNI, *who weighs it in his hand, and lets it fall on the pavement with a dull thud.*]

It is yours; it is the head
Of Montagna dei Parcitadi; take it.
It is for your saddle bow,
For you to carry with you to Gadara
And leave it with our father, and say to him:

"Malatestino sends you
This token, lest you doubt his guardianship,
And pledges you his word
He will not let the prisoner escape;
And asks you in return
The three foot black white-spotted horse you said
That you would give him,
With saddle set with gold."
How hot it is!

[*He wipes the sweat from his forehead.* GIANCIOTTO *has seated himself again at the table.*]

I tell you,
When the light struck upon his eyes, he snorted,
As a horse does when it shies. Give me to drink.

[*He drains a cup that stands full.* GIANCIOTTO *seems gloomy, and chews in silence, without swallowing, like an ox ruminating. The slayer of* MONTAGNA *sits where* FRANCESCA *had been sitting. The blood-stained bundle lies on the pavement; through the window can be seen the sun as it sets behind the Apennines, crimsoning the peaks and the clouds.*]

You are not wroth with me?
You did not want to have us wait a year
In hopes of ransom from the Perdecittade?
I tell you we should not have had the ransom,
Sure as a florin's yellow.
From this day backwards
The Malatesti never have given quarter,
Since they first cut their teeth.
It is not two months now, at Cesena, our father

Just saved his skin by a mere miracle
From the clutches of Corrado Montefeltvo,
And the bastard Filipuccio is still living!
Heaven bless and save
Frate Alberigo,
Who knows full well the way to spare at once
Both trunk and branches!
It is time now for every Ghibelline
To come to his desert,
As the gay Knight would have us.

[*He takes the sword lying across the table, and strikes the scabbard with his hand.*]

And here is the dessert for every feast
Of peace and amity.
Do not be wroth with me,
Giovanni, I am yours.
Are you not called the Lamester
And am I not the One-eyed? . . .

[*He is silent an instant, deceitfully.*]

But Paolo is the Beautiful!

[GIANCIOTTO *lifts his head and gazes fixedly at* MALATESTINO. *In the silence is heard the jingling of his spurs as he moves his foot restlessly on the floor.*]

GIANCIOTTO.

You are a babbler too?

[MALATESTINO *is about to pour out more wine. His brother arrests his hand.*]

No, do not drink,
But answer me. What is it you have done
To vex Francesca?
What have you done to her?

MALATESTINO.

I! What is it she says?

GIANCIOTTO.

You have changed colour.

MALATESTINO.

What is it she says?

GIANCIOTTO.

Answer me now!

MALATESTINO.

[*Pretending to be confused.*]

I cannot answer you.

GIANCIOTTO.

What do you harbour against her in your mind?

MALATESTINO

[*With a gleam in his eye*].

She told you this? And did she not change colour
While she was saying it?

GIANCIOTTO.

Enough, Malatestino!
Look at me in the eyes.
I limp in going, but I go straight before me.
You go a crooked way, and you smooth out
The sound your feet have made. Only, take heed
I do not set my hand upon you. There
You would writhe your best in vain.
So now I say to you:
Woe to you if you touch my lady! You,
You should know, having seen me at the work,
That a less time it is

Between the touch of the spur and the first leap
Of the Barbary horse
Than between my saying and doing. Think of it.

MALATESTINO

[*In a low voice, with downcast eye*].

And if the brother sees that there is one
That touches of a truth his brother's wife,
And is incensed at it, and stirs himself
To wipe the shame out, does he therefore sin?
And if, for this, he is accused to have
Harboured ill thought against the woman, say:
Is the accusation just?

[GIANCIOTTO *springs up and raises his fists as if to crush the youth. But he restrains himself, his arms fall.*]

GIANCIOTTO

Malatestino, scourge of hell, if you
Would have me not put out
The other eye by which your blinking soul
Offends the world, speak now,
And tell me what it is that you have seen.

[MALATESTINO *rises and goes with his silent, cat-like steps to the door near the table. He listens for some instants; then opens the door suddenly with a swift movement, and looks. He sees no one. He goes back to his brother's side.*

Speak.

MALATESTINO.

Not for threats. You frighten me, I say.
Because I wore no visor, I was made
Blind of one eye; but you must wear indoors

Visor and headpiece, chin-piece, eye-piece, all
Of tempered steel, without a flaw in it!
You will see nothing, nothing can come through
The iron-barred approaches to your brain.

GIANCIOTTO.

Come, come, the thing! None of your talk! The thing!
Tell me what you have seen! Tell me the man!

MALATESTINO.

Were you nowise surprised
When some one who had gone away from here
No later than December, suddenly
Gave up his post at Florence
And was already back by February?

[*One of the silver cups is heard to crack, as it is crushed in* GIANCIOTTO'S *hand.*]

GIANCIOTTO.

Paolo? No, no. It is not.

[*He rises, leaves the table, and walks to and fro in the room, grimly, with overclouded eyes. He stumbles against the blood-stained bundle. He goes towards the window, whose panes glitter in the light of the setting sun. He sits down on the window-seat, and takes his head between his hands, as if to collect his thoughts.* MALATESTINO *plays with the sword, drawing it half in and half out of the scabbard.*]

Malatestino, here!

[*The youth comes across to him swiftly, almost without sound, as if his feet were shod with felt.* GIANCIOTTO *enfolds him in his arms, and holds him tightly between his armoured knees, and speaks to him breath to breath.*]

Are you sure? Have you seen this?

MALATESTINO.

Yes.

GIANCIOTTO.

How and when?

MALATESTINO.

I have seen him often enter . . .

GIANCIOTTO.

Enter where?

MALATESTINO.

Enter the room.

GIANCIOTTO.

Well? That is not enough.
He is a kinsman. They might talk together.
There are the women . . . You have seen him go
With the musicians, it may be . . .

MALATESTINO.

At night.
For God's sake, do not hurt me! Not so hard!
You have your iron gauntlets. Let me go.

[*He writhes in his grasp.*]

GIANCIOTTO.

Have I heard right? You said . . .
Say it again.

MALATESTINO.

At night,
At night, I say, I have seen him.

GIANCIOTTO.

If you should lie, I will break
Your body in two.

MALATESTINO.

At night,
I have seen him enter, and go out at dawn.
You were in arms against the Urbinati.

GIANCIOTTO.

I will break you, if you lie.

MALATESTINO.

Would you like to see and feel?

GIANCIOTTO.

I must do so.
If you have any will to go alive
Out of these mortal pincers.

MALATESTINO.

Then, to-night?

GIANCIOTTO.

To-night, then.

MALATESTINO.

But can you find out the way
To cheat, to smile? Ah, no, you cannot smile.

GIANCIOTTO.

Let my revenge teach me the way to smile,
If my delight could never.

MALATESTINO.

Can you kiss
Both, one after the other, and not bite
Instead?

GIANCIOTTO.

Yes, I will kiss them, thinking them
Already dead.

MALATESTINO.

You must put both your arms
About them, you must talk to them, and not
Tremble.

GIANCIOTTO.

Ah, you are playing with my sorrow!
Beware! it has two edges.

MALATESTINO.

Do not hurt me,
For God's sake!

GIANCIOTTO.

Good; but tell me how you think:
The way, and speedily.

MALATESTINO.

You must take your leave,
And go from here, take horse, and by the gate
Of San Genesio with all your escort
Set out for Pesaro. I will come with you.
You will say you are wroth with me
For the Parcitade's head's sake, and desire
To take me to our father at Gradara,
That he may punish me or pardon me.
So they will think
That they are left alone. Do you understand?
Then, half-way through the night,
We will leave the escort, and come back again,
And enter by the gate of the Gattolo
Before the moon is up. We will give the signal
To Rizio. But let me dispose of that.
Saddle your swiftest horse, and take with you
A little linen
To bind about his hoofs, in case of need,

Because at night the stones
Upon the noisy way
May well be traitors, brother.

GIANCIOTTO.

Then shall I see?
You are sure? Then I shall take them in the act . . . .

MALATESTINO.

Not so hard! Now I think,
There is the slave, there is the Cyprian slave . . . .
She is their go-between.
Sly is she, works with charms . . . .
I have seen her as she goes
Snuffing the wind. . . . I must find a way to lead her
Into a snare, and blindfold her. But this,
Leave this to me: you need not think of anything
Till you are at the door.

GIANCIOTTO.

On your life now, shall I take them in the act?

MALATESTINO.

Enough of this, by God!
Let me go, now, let me go! I am not
Your prey.
[*Through the door is heard the voice of* PAOLO.]

PAOLO

[*Outside*].
Where is Giovanni?

[GIANCIOTTO *lets* MALATESTINO *go, and rises with a white face.*]

MALATESTINO.

Look to it now,
Look to it; no suspicion!

[*As* PAOLO *opens the door and enters,* MALATESTINO *pretends to be angry with* GIANCIOTTO.]

Ah, at last
You have let me go!

[*He pretends to suffer in his wrists.*]

By God, it is well for you
You were born my elder brother, otherwise. . . .
Ah, Paolo, well met!

[PAOLO *wears a long rich surtout falling below his knees nearly to the ankle, girt at the waist by a jewelled belt through which is thrust a beautiful damascened dagger. His curled hair, not parted, but waving in a mass, surrounds his face like a cloud.*]

PAOLO.

What is the matter?

MALATESTINO.

See,
Giovanni is enraged
Because I have lost all patience at the last
And have struck dumb Montagna, being weary
Of listening to his cries (Francesca too
Could get no sleep) and weary too of hearing
My father say twice over,
By word of mouth and message;
"Will you keep watch on him?
Are you sure you can keep watch?
I know he will escape;

I know that you will let him go, and then,
When he has gone, you will not bring him back!"
By God, I was tired of it. There is his head.

PAOLO.

You cut it off yourself?

MALATESTINO.

Yes, I myself,
And neatly.

[PAOLO *looks at the bundle, but draws back so as not to stain himself with the dripping blood.*]

Ah, you draw back, it seems
You fear to stain your garments?
I did not know I had
Two sisters, both so dainty!

GIANCIOTTO.

Enough of jesting! Paolo,
I have to take him with me to Gradara,
To our father; he must plead
His cause himself,
For disobeying. What do you say to it?

PAOLO.

I say that it is well for him to go,
Giovanni.

MALATESTINO.

I am content.
But I must bear the token;
I will hang it to my saddle: that is staunch.

[*He takes up the bundle by the cord.*]

I have no fear our father will be angry.
He will be filled with joy,

I tell you, when the knots are all untied.
And he will give me the black horse for war,
And maybe the grey jennet for the chase.

GIANCIOTTO.

Get ready then, and without lingering,
It is already evening.

[MALATESTINO *takes up the bundle to carry it away.*]

PAOLO

[*To* GIOVANNI].

I see your men are armed at front and back,
And wait the clarion.

[*The two brothers go towards the window lit up by the sunset, and sit down.*]

MALATESTINO

[*Going*].

Ah, but how heavy! and without a helmet!
The Parcitadi always were gross oxen,
Fatted for slaughtering, great horned heads.
Ah, Paozzo, where you go
You leave behind a scent of orange-water.
Take care, a drop may drip upon your clothes.

[*He goes out.*]

PAOLO.

He is all teeth and claws, ready for biting.
Our men at arms used once
To say he always slept with one eye closed
And one eye open, even in his sleep.
Now I believe he never sleeps at all,
Nor slacks the sinews of his cruelty.
He was made to conquer lands, and die some day

Of extreme cold, God keep him, our good brother!
So you are Podestà of Pesaro!
Our father from Gradara scans the hill
Of Pesaro as if he watched his prey.
You, with your strength and wisdom,
Should give it to him soon,
Giovanni.

GIANCIOTTO.

It is not a year yet since
You went to Florence, Captain of the People,
And now I go as Podestà Not long
You stayed at Florence. I shall stay there long,
Because it is not well for me to yield
The office to another. Yet to leave
Francesca for so long,
Goes to my heart a little.

PAOLO.

You can come back again from time to time,
Pesaro is not far.

GIANCIOTTO.

The Podestà is not allowed to leave
His post, so long as lasts
His office, as you know, nor bring with him
His wife. But I will leave her in your care,
Brother, my most dear wife; you will be here.

PAOLO.

I have held her always
As a dear sister might be held.

GIANCIOTTO.

I know,
Paolo.

PAOLO.

Be very sure
That I will guard her for you well.

GIANCIOTTO.

I know,
Paolo. You from Ravenna
Brought her a virgin to your brother's bed
And you will keep her for me from all harm.

PAOLO.

I will tell Orabile
To leave Ghaggiolo and come
To Rimino to keep her company.

GIANCIOTTO.

See that they love each other, Paolo,
For they are kinswomen.

PAOLO.

Francesca often
Sends gifts to her.

GIANCIOTTO.

Go, call her. It is late.
The sun has set, and I shall have to rest
A little at Gradara,
And yet be at the gates
Of Pesaro before the third hour. Go,
Go you yourself and call her. She has gone
Back to her room, because Malatestino
Frighted her with his cruelty. Go you,
Comfort her, tell her not to be afraid
Of being left alone, and call her here.

[*He rises and puts his hand lightly on his brother's shoulder as if to urge him.* PAOLO *goes towards the door.* GIOVANNI *stands motionless, and follow him with murderous eyes. As he goes out,* GIOVANNI *stretches out his hand as if to swear an oath. Then he moves towards the table, and takes up the cracked cup, wishing to hide it. He turns, sees the little barred door still open, throws the cup into the darkness, and closes the door. At the other door* FRANCESCA *appears by the side of* PAOLO.]

FRANCESCA.

Pardon me, my dear lord,
If I have left you hastily. You know
The reason.

GIANCIOTTO.

My dear lady, I know well
The reason, and I am sorry
That you have had to suffer by the fault
Of this sad brother. And I go to see
Both to your peace and to his punishment,
For I intend to take him to our father,
For judgment at Gradara. He prepares
Already to set forth. Within a little
We shall have left the city.

FRANCESCA.

He will bear
Ill-will against me, if you should accuse him
Before his father. Pardon him, I pray.
He is a boy.

GIANCIOTTO.

Yet, lady, it is better,
For your sake, that he comes with me. I leave
Paolo with you. Trust Paolo. His Orabile

Will come to stay with you at Rimino,
And keep you company: he promises.
Often from Pesaro
I mean to send you messages, and hope
Often to have the like from Rimino.

FRANCESCA.

Surely, my lord. You need not fear for me.

GIANCIOTTO.

Put every trouble freely from your mind,
Let songs and music give you joy, and have
Beautiful robes, and lovely odours. Not
To Guido's daughter suits the spinning wheel.
I know it. And I say
My mother's saying but to make you smile.
You are not angry with me?

FRANCESCA.

In your saying
There seems to lie secret rebuke for me,
My lord.

GIANCIOTTO.

A good old saying, that was born
Within the dark walls of Verrucchio,
That now are grown too narrow to hem in
The Malatesi in our house to-day.
If any spin, they spin
Only the purple, and with golden distaffs.
Come to my arms, my most dear lady!

[FRANCESCA *goes up to him; he takes her in his arms and kisses her.* PAOLO *stands silent in the doorway.*]

Now
I have to say farewell. Never so fair

You seemed to me, never so sweet. And yet
I leave you.

[*He smooths her hair with his hand; then looses her.*]

O, my brother,
Keep her in safety and heaven keep you both.
Come, and pledge faith with me.

[PAOLO *goes up to him, and they embrace.*]

Where is my gorget?

FRANCESCA.

Here it is.

[*She gives it to him.*]

GIANCIOTTO

[*Putting it on*].

Paolo, buckle it for me.

[PAOLO *buckles it on.* FRANCESCA *hands him the basnet.*]

Do you remember, brother,
That night before the Mastra Tower, that bolt
Out of a crossbow? You,
Francesca, do you remember?
It was at just this hour.
Cignatta was killed then. To-day Montagna
Joins him. 'Tis not a year.
The house is silent now; then, all the towers
Were crackling to the sky.

[FRANCESCA *takes the sword from the table and buckles his sword-belt.*]

Francesca, do you remember? Then you gave us

Wine, Scian wine, to drink. We drank together
Out of one cup.

[*He is fully armed.*]

Now let me drink again!

FRANCESCA.

One of the cups is missing. There were two.
Where is the other?

[*She looks to see if it has fallen.*]

GIANCIOTTO.

One will do for us
Still.

[*He pours out the wine and offers it to* FRANCESCA.]

And good luck God give you!

FRANCESCA.

I cannot drink
This wine, my lord. I am not used to it.

GIANCIOTTO.

Drink as you drank then, and pass on the cup
That your kinsman may drink also, as he drank then.

[FRANCESCA *drinks and offers the cup to* PAOLO, *who takes it.*]

PAOLO.

Good luck to the Podestà of Pesaro!

[*He drinks throwing back his curled head. Through the door is heard the voice of* MALATESTINO, *who throws open the door, and appears in full armour. From the court is heard the sound of bugles.*]

MALATESTINO.

Ready, Giovanni? Hark, the clarion!
To horse! To horse!

ACT V.

The room with the curtained alcove, the musicians' gallery, the lectern with the book closed. Four waxen torches burn in the iron candlestick; two tapers on the small table. The compartments of the long window are almost all open to the peaceful night air. The pot of basil is on the window-sill, and beside it is a gilt plate heaped with bunches of early grapes.

[FRANCESCA *is seen through the half-drawn curtains of the alcove, lying on the bed, on which she has laid herself without undressing. The* WOMEN, *who wear white fillets, are seated on low stools; they speak quietly, so as not to disturb their mistress. Near them, on a stool, are laid five silver lamps, which have gone out.*]

ADONELLA.

She has fallen asleep. She dreams.

[BIANCOFIORE *rises and goes softly up to the alcove, looks, then turns, and goes back to her seat.*]

BIANCOFIORE.

How beautiful she is!

ALTICHIARA.

Summer is come; she grows
In beauty with the summer.

ALDA,

Like ears of corn.

GARSENDA.

And like
Poppies.

BIANCOFIORE.

O, beautiful
Summer, go not away !
The nights begin to grow a little cool.
Do you feel the breeze ?

ALDA.

It comes
From the sea. Oh, the delight!

[*With her face to the window, she draws in a long breath*]

ADONELLA.

Lord Autumn comes our way
With grass and figs in his lap.

BIANCOFIORE.

September! Grape and fig begin to droop.

ALTICHIARA

[*Pointing to the plate*].

Here, Adonella, take
A bunch of grapes to strip.

ADONELLA.

You are too greedy.

ALTICHIARA.

Come, come, your mouth is watering for them.

[ADONELLA *takes a bunch of grapes from the plate, and goes back to her seat, holding the bunch in the air, while the others strip it of its grapes.*]

BIANCOFIORE.

It is like sweet muscatel.

ALDA.

Don't throw away the skin!

ALTICHIARA.

It is all good to eat, kernel and skin.

GARSENDA.

Here is a bitter kernel.

BIANCOFIORE.

Grown on the shady side.

ADONELLA.

How still it is!

ALDA.

How tranquil!

GARSENDA.

Listen! I hear a galley
Weigh anchor.

BIANCOFIORE.

For to-night
Madonna has no singing.

ALTICHIARA.

She is weary.

ALDA.

Why does the prisoner
Cry out no more?

GARSENDA.

Messer Malatestino has cut off
His head.

ALDA.

Is that the truth?

GARSENDA.

The truth; to-day, at Vespers.

ALDA.

How do you know?

GARSENDA.

Smaragdi told it me,
And had seen him, too,
Tie something huddled in a cloth to his saddle,
When, with Messer Giovanni
He mounted in the court. It was the head,
The prisoner's head.

ADONELLA.

Where do they carry it?

ALTICHIARA.

To whom do they carry it?

BIANCOFIORE.

Now they are riding
By the sea shore,
Under the stars,
They and the murdered
Head!

ADONELLA.

Where will they have come?

ALDA.

They should have come
To hell, and stayed there!

GARSENDA.

One can breathe in the house
Now they are here no longer,
The lame man and the blind man!

ALTICHIARA.

Hush! hush! let not Madonna
Hear you.

GARSENDA.

She is hardly breathing.

ALDA.

Messer Paolo
Is back again?

ALTICHIARA.

Hush!

[FRANCESCA *groans in her sleep*].

ADONELLA.

She is wakening.

[*She throws the grape-stalk out of the window.* BIANCOFIORE *again rises, and goes up to the alcove, and looks.*]

BIANCOFIORE.

No,
She is not awake; she is crying in her sleep.

ADONELLA.

She is dreaming.

ALDA.

O Garsenda, does she know
The prisoner is not crying any more
Because they have cut his head off?

GARSENDA.

Certainly
She knows.

BIANCOFIORE.

Perhaps she is dreaming of it now.

ADONELLA.

We must sit up to-night,
Who knows to what hour?

ALDA.

Are you sleepy, Adonella?

ALTICHIARA.

Simonetto, the fifer, is waiting on the stairs!

ADONELLA.

Who waits for you, then? Suzzo, the falconer,
With lure of pretty leather?

ALDA.

Hush! She is wakening.

BIANCOFIORE.

And did it bleed, Garsenda?

GARSENDA.

Bleed? What?

BIANCOFIORE.

That bundle at the saddle-bow?

GARSENDA.

I saw but dimly, for the court was dark.
But this I know : Smaragdi had to wash
The pavement, there, in the hall.

BIANCOFIORE.

Now they are nearing the Cattolica.

GARSENDA.

God keep them far away, and let them never
Find their way back again!

BIANCOFIORE.

Think of the frightened horse
Feeling the dead thing dangle in the night!

ADONELLA.

How sweetly the sweet basil smells by night!

ALTICHIARA.

How thick it grows; the pot
No longer holds it.

BIANCOFIORE.

You know, Garsenda, tell us
The story of Lisabetta of Messina,
That loved a youth of Pisa, and how her brothers
Killed him in secret, and she found his body
And cut the head away
From off the shoulders, set it in a pot,
And earth with it, and planted
A sprig of basil plant,
And watered it with her tears,
And saw it blossom so, out of her weeping.
Tell us, Garsenda, very quietly
While we are waiting.

[FRANCESCA *gives a deeper groan, and turns as if half stifled on the bed. The* WOMEN *shiver.*]

ALDA.

Listen,
She is crying in her sleep. It is some bad dream.

GARSENDA.

She is sleeping on her back; the nightmare weighs
Upon her breast.

ALTICHIARA.

Shall we awake her?

BIANCOFIORE.

Evil
It is too suddenly
To rouse the heart that sees.
How should we know
What truth she sees revealed?

ADONELLA.

The Slave interprets all her dreams to her.

[FRANCESCA *utters a cry of terror, springs from the bed, and seems in the act to fly from some savage pursuit, throwing out her hands as if to unloose herself from some grasp.*]

FRANCESCA.

No, no, it is not I, it is not I!
Ah, ah, they seize me with their teeth! Help! help!
They snatch my heart. Help, help!
Paolo!

[*She shudders, stops, and turns on herself, pale, and breathing with difficulty, while her* WOMEN *surround her in consternation, trying to comfort her.*]

GARSENDA.

Madonna, Madonna, we are here, see, see,
We are here, Madonna.

ALTICHIARA.

Do not be afraid!

ADONELLA.

There is no one here; there is no one here but we,
Madonna. No one is harming you, Madonna,

FRANCESCA

[*Shivering*].

What have I said? Did I call?
O God, what have I done?

ALDA.

You have had some discomfortable dream,
Madonna.

GARSENDA.

Now it is finished. We are here.
All's quiet.

FRANCESCA.

Is it late?

BIANCOFIORE.

The sweat is standing out upon your forehead.

[*She wipes it off.*]

FRANCESCA.

Is it night yet? Garsenda,
Biancofiore, Alda, you are all in white.

GARSENDA.

It might perhaps be four hours after midnight,
Madonna.

FRANCESCA.

Have I slept so long? Smaragdi,
Where is Smaragdi?
She has not come back yet?

BIANCOFIORE.

She has not come back.

FRANCESCA.

Why has she not come back?

BIANCOFIORE

When did you send her,
Madonna?

FRANCESCA.

Are you not mistaken? Sleep,
Perhaps, deceived you, and you did not see her
When she came in.

GARSENDA.

Madonna,
No, none of us closed eyelid;
We watched beside you all the night.

ADONELLA.

Perhaps
She has come back, and waits, as she is wont
Lying without the door.

FRANCESCA.

Look out and see,
Adonella, see if she is there.

[ADONELLA *draws back the folds of the curtain opens the door, and looks out.*]

ADONELLA.

Smaragdi!
Smaragdi! There is no answer.
No one is there. It is all dark.

FRANCESCA.

But call,
Call her again.

ADONELLA.

Smaragdi!

FRANCESCA.

Take a light.

[GARSENDA *takes one of the lamps, lights it at a taper, and goes to the door. She and her companion look around.*]

She should have been here now some time ago.
What harm can have befallen her? God knows what;
It can be no good thing.

BIANCOFIORE.

You have not yet
Come quite out of the horror of the dream,
Madonna.

ALTICHIARA.

Breathe the air, the night is fresh,
The night is still.

FRANCESCA.

The moon
Is risen?

ALDA.

It must be rising on the hills,
But there is yet no dawn upon the sea.

[ADONELLA *and* GARSENDA *re-enter. One of them puts out the lamp.*]

FRANCESCA

[*anxiously*].

Well? Is she there?

GARSENDA.

Madonna, there is no one.

ADONELLA.

Nothing but silence
And darkness everywhere; the whole house sleeps.

GARSENDA.

We only saw . . .

[*She hesitates.*]

FRANCESCA.

You only saw . . . whom did you see?

GARSENDA

[*hesitating*].

Madonna,

Some one was there . . . some one was standing there,
Leaning against the wall . . .
Still as a statue . . . all alone . . . his girdle
Shining . . . Madonna, do not be afraid . . .

[*Goes near to her and lowers her voice.*]

It was Messer Paolo!

FRANCESCA

[*startled*].

O, why?

ADONELLA.

Madonna
Will have her hair made ready for the night?

FRANCESCA.

No, no, I am not sleepy. I will wait.

BIANCOFIORE.

Her shoes unloosed?

ALDA.

The perfumes ?

FRANCESCA.

I will wait
A little more. I am no longer sleepy.
I will wait until Smaragdi comes.

ALTICHIARA.

Let me go
And seek her.

GARSENDA.

The poor thing is tired perhaps,
At the day's end, and sleeps where she has dropped.
Perhaps she is lying now
Upon the stairs.

FRANCESCA.

Go, go, and I will read
Till you return. Bring me a taper, Alda.

[ALDA *takes a taper and fixes it at the head of the reading-desk.*]

Go now. You are all in white!
The Summer is not dead?
When it was evening, did you see the swallows
Begin to fly away?
I was elsewhere,
I was looking on the hills,
When the sun set to-night.
They have not all flown yet, have they? But perhaps
To-morrow all the other flocks will follow.
I will go up on the tower, to see them go,
And you will sing me a merry song, men dance to,
As if 'twere the March calends. Have you still
The flight of swallows painted, as you had?

ALDA.

Yes, Madonna.

FRANCESCA.

To-morrow at the dance
You will put on
Over these white
Dresses a vest of black.
You will be like
"The creature of delight."

BIANCOFIORE.

Yes, Madonna.

FRANCESCA.

Go, go!

[*She opens the book.*]

[*Each of the* WOMEN *takes her silver lamp, which swings from a curved handle. First* ADONELLA *goes to the tall candlestick, and, standing on tiptoe, lights her lamp at one of the torches. She bows, and goes out, while* FRANCESCA *follows her with her eyes.*]

Go, too, Adonella!

[GARSENDA *does the same.*]

And you, Garsenda.

[ALTICHIARA *does the same.*]

And you, too, Altichiara.

[ALDA *does the same.*]

And you, Alda.

[*The four have gone out, one by one.* BIANCOFIORE *remains, and she also is about to light her lamp, but as she is shorter than the others, she cannot reach the flame.*]

Oh, Biancofiore, what a little one!

You will not ever reach to light your lamp.
You are the gentlest of them. Little dove,

[BIANCOFIORE *turns smiling.*]

Come!

[BIANCOFIORE *goes up to her.* FRANCESCA *caresses her hair.*]

It is all of gold. You are, I think,
A little like my sister; you remember her,
Samaritana?

BIANCOFIORE.

Yes, indeed, Madonna.
Such sweetness cannot be forgot. I have her
Here, in my heart, with the angels.

FRANCESCA.

She was sweet,
My sister; was she not sweet, Biancofiore?
Ah, if she were but here, if she might make
Her little bed beside my bed to-night!
If I might hear again
Her little naked feet run to the window,
If I might hear her run with naked feet,
My little dove, and say, and say to me:
"Francesca, now the morning-star is born,
And it has chased away the Pleiades!"

BIANCOFIORE.

You weep, Madonna.

FRANCESCA.

You tremble, Biancofiore.
She too was frightened of a sudden; I heard
Her heart beat; and she said to me: "O sister,
Listen to me: stay with me still, O stay
With me! we were born here:

Do not forsake me!"
And I said to her: "O take me,
And let me be with you,
And let one covering cover us!"

BIANCOFIORE.

O Madonna,
Your words pierce through my heart,
What melancholy holds you
Still?

FRANCESCA.

No, no, do not weep:
Gentle you are. But come, light your lamp here.

BIANCOFIORE.

May I not stay with you? May I not sleep
Here, at the foot of the bed?

FRANCESCA.

No, Biancofiore. Light your lamp, and go,
And God go with you. Now Samaritana,
It may be, is thinking of her sister.

[BIANCOFIORE *lights her lamp at the taper, and bends to kiss* FRANCESCA'S *hand.*]

Go,
Go, do not weep. Let all sad thoughts go by.
To-morrow you shall sing to me. Now go.

[BIANCOFIORE *turns and walks slowly towards the door. As she is going out,* FRANCESCA *gives way to her presentiment.*]

You are not going, Biancofiore?

BIANCOFIORE.

No,
I will stay with you, Madonna. Let me stay
At least until Smaragdi has come back.

FRANCESCA

[*Hesitates an instant*].

Go!

BIANCOFIORE.

God keep you, Madonna.

[*She goes out, closing the door behind her.*]

[*Left alone,* FRANCESCA *makes several steps towards the door; then stands still, listening.*]

FRANCESCA.

And let it be so if it is my fate.

[*Goes resolutely up to the door.*]

I will call him.

[*Hesitates and draws back.*]

He is still there, and he stands
Leaning against the wall;
Still as a statue, all alone; his girdle
Shining in the shadow. Who said that to me?
Who was it? Was it not said long ago?
Within the helmet all the face like fire . . .

[*Visions pass before her soul in a flash.*]

He is silent, and the lances
Of the spearmen round him.
He stands, and the arrow whistles through his hair.
He is cleansed from the pollution of the guile.
He drains the long draught, throwing back his head.

Ah, now all's gone again!
The enemy holds fast
The secret and the sword.
" The executioner
I make me of your will."
But iron shall not divide the lips, but flame
Shall not divide the lips.

[*She wanders to and fro, wretched and feverish.*]

The utmost flame of fire shall not divide them.

[*She takes up the silver mirror and looks at herself in it.*]

O silence, and still water, sepulchre,
Pale sepulchre of my face!
What is this voice that says
I never was more beautiful than now?
"And in the solitude that was on fire
With your eyes, I have lived
With so swift energy,
Travailing secretly" . . . .
One voice alone cries out
On the topmost of my heart,
And all the blood flies . . . . Ah!

[*She starts, hearing a light knocking at the door. She puts down the mirror, blows out the taper with a breath, goes to the door, tottering, and calls, in a low voice.*]

Smaragdi! Smaragdi!

PAOLO

[*Voice heard*].

Francesca!

[*She flings the door open vehemently. With a craving as of thirst she throws herself into the arms of her lover.*]

FRANCESCA.

Paolo! Paolo!

[*He is dressed as at Vespers; his head is bare.*]

PAOLO.

Life of my life, never was my desire
So ardent for you. In my heart I felt
A dying down
Of the bright spirits that live within your eyes.
My forces ebbed away into the night,
Out of my breast, a flood
Terrible, clangorous,
And fear took hold upon my soul, as when
In that sealed hour,
You put me to the test, God witnessing,
The test of the arrow,
And raised me there whither although he wills it
No man returns by willing to return.
Is it not morning, is it not morning yet?
The stars have all gone down into your hair,
Scattered about the confines of the shades,
Where life may never find them!

[*He kisses her hair passionately again and again.*]

FRANCESCA.

Pardon me,
Pardon me! Far away
You come before me,
Far off and silent,
With fixed, dry eyeballs, as upon that day
Between the inflexible lances of the fight.
A hard sleep falling on me like a blow
Scattered my soul
As a stem breaks, and then I seemed to lie

Lost on the stones. And then there came to
me
The dream that long while now
I have seen in sleep, the strange
Dream that has tortured me;
And I was full of many terrors, full
Of terrors; and my women
Saw me, and how I trembled,
And how I wept . . .

PAOLO.

O, wept!

FRANCESCA.

Pardon me, pardon me,
Sweet friend! You have awakened me from
sleep,
Freed me from every anguish.
It is not morning yet,
The stars have not gone down into the sea,
The summer is not over, and you are mine,
And I, I am all yours,
And this is perfect joy
The passion of the ardour of our life.

[PAOLO *kisses her insatiably.*]

PAOLO.

You shivered?

FRANCESCA.

See, the door
Is open, and there passes
The breath of the night. Do you not feel it
too?
This is the hour,
The hour of silence,

That sheds the dew of night
Upon the manes
Of horses on the roads.
But shut the door.

[PAOLO *shuts the door.*]

Paolo, did you see with your own eyes
The horsemen as they went away?

PAOLO.

Yes, yes,
I watched them from the tower, for a long while
Until the last lance faded
Into the dark, and I could see no more.
Come, come, Francesca! Many hours of gladness
We have before us,
With the wild melody of unknown winds
And the swift ravishment of solitude
In fire, and the violent
River without a goal,
And the immortal thirst;
But now this hour that flies
Fills me with lust to live
A thousand lives,
In the quiver of the air that kisses you,
In the short breath of the sea,
In the fury of the world,
That not one thing
Of all the infinite things
That are in you
Lie hid from me,
And I die not before I have ploughed up
Out of your depths

And relished to its infinite root in you
My perfect joy.

[*He draws her towards the cushions by the windows.*]

FRANCESCA.

Kiss me upon my eyes, upon my brow,
Upon my cheeks, my throat,
So . . .so . . .
Stay, and my wrists, my fingers . . .
So . . . so . . . And take my soul and pour it out,
Because the breath of the night
Turns back my soul again
To things of long ago,
And the low voices of the night turn back
My soul to things that were,
And joys enjoyed are they that now weigh down
My heart, and as you were
I see you still, and not as you shall be,
My fair friend, my sweet friend.

PAOLO.

I will carry you where all things are forgot,
And no more time made slave
Is lord of our desire.
Then shall the day and night
Be mingled even as one
Upon the earth as upon one sole pillow;
Then shall the hands of dawn
No more unclasp from one another's holding
The dusky arms and the white arms of them,
Nor yet untwist
The tangles of their hair and veins.

FRANCESCA.

It says
Here in the book, here where you have not read:
" We have been one life; it were a seemly thing
That we be also one death."

PAOLO.

Let the book
Be closed!

[*He rises, closes the book on the reading desk, and blows out the taper.*]

And read in it no more. Not there
Our destiny is written, but in the stars,
That palpitate above
As your throat palpitates,
Your wrists, your brow,
Perhaps because they were your garland once,
Your necklet when you went
Burningly through the ways of heaven? From what
Vineyard of earth were these grapes gathered in?
They have the smell
Of drunkenness and honey,
They are like veins, they are swollen with delight,
Fruits of the night! The flaming feet of Love
Shall tread them in the winepress. Give me your mouth
Again! again!

[FRANCESCA *lies back on the cushions, forgetful of everything. All at once, in the dead silence, a violent shock is heard on the door, as if some one hurled himself against it. The lovers start up in terror, and rise to their feet.*]

THE VOICE OF GIANCIOTTO.

Francesca, open! Francesca!

[*The* WOMAN *is petrified with terror.* PAOLO *looks round the room, putting his hand to his dagger. He catches sight of the bolt of the trap-door.*]

PAOLO

[*In a low voice*].

Take heart, take heart, Francesca! I will get down
By the way of the trap-door.
Go, go, and open to him.
But do not tremble.

[*He lifts the trap-door. The door seems to quiver at the repeated blows.*]

THE VOICE OF GIANCIOTTO.

Open, Francesca, open!

PAOLO.

Open to him! Go now.
I wait beneath. If he but touches you
Cry out and I am with you.
Go boldly, do not tremble!

[*He begins to go down, while the* WOMAN *in obedience to him, goes to open the door, tottering.*]

THE VOICE OF GIANCIOTTO.

Open! upon your life, Francesca, open!

[*The door being opened* GIANCIOTTO, *armed, and covered with dust, rushes furiously into the room, looking for his brother in every direction. Suddenly he catches sight of* PAOLO, *standing head and shoulders above the level of the floor, struggling to free himself from the bolt of the trap-door, which has caught in a corner of his cloak.* FRANCESCA *utters a piercing cry, while* GIANCIOTTO *falls upon his brother, seizing him by the hair, and forcing him to come up.*

GIANCIOTTO.

So, you are caught in a trap,
Traitor! They are good to have you by the hair,
Your ringlets!

FRANCESCA
[*rushing forward*].

Let him go!
Let him go! Me, take me!

[*The husband loosens his hold.* PAOLA *springs up on the other side of the trap-door, and unsheathes his dagger.* GIANCIOTTO, *drawing back, bares his sword, and rushes upon him with terrible force.* FRANCESCA *throws herself between the two men; but as her husband has leant all his weight on the blow, and is unable to draw back, her breast is pierced by the sword, she staggers, turns on herself, towards* PAOLA, *who lets fall his dagger, and catches her in his arms.*]

FRANCESCA
[*dying*].

Ah, Paolo!

[GIANCIOTTO *pauses for an instant. He sees the woman clasped in the arms of her lover, who seals her expiring life with his lips. Mad with rage and sorrow, he pierces his brother's side with another deadly thrust. The two bodies sway to and fro for an instant without a sound. Then, still linked together, they fall at full length on the pavement.* GIANCIOTTO *stoops in silence, bends his knee with a painful effort, and, across the other knee, breaks his blood-stained sword.*]

Lightning Source UK Ltd.
Milton Keynes UK
UKHW010239241220
375731UK00002B/457

9 781434 433794